T0158858

THE PRESENCE OF GOD, FROM GARDEN TO TABLE

A Bible Study in the Language of Food

Londie Phillips with Kristine DeBaca

WESTBOW
PRESS®
A DIVISION OF THOMAS NELSON
& ZONDERVAN

Scripture quotations marked (NIV) are taken from the Holy Bible, New International Version®, NIV®. Copyright © 1973, 1978, 1984, 2011 by Biblica, Inc.™ Used by permission of Zondervan. All rights reserved worldwide. www. zondervan.com The "NIV" and "New International Version" are trademarks registered in the United States Patent and Trademark Office by Biblica, Inc.™

Scripture quotations marked (KJV) are taken from the King James Version.

Photography by Londie Phillips

This book is a work of non-fiction. Unless otherwise noted, the author and the publisher make no explicit guarantees as to the accuracy of the information contained in this book and in some cases, names of people and places have been altered to protect their privacy.

WestBow Press books may be ordered through booksellers or by contacting:

WestBow Press
A Division of Thomas Nelson & Zondervan
1663 Liberty Drive
Bloomington, IN 47403
www.westbowpress.com
1 (866) 928-1240

Because of the dynamic nature of the Internet, any web addresses or links contained in this book may have changed since publication and may no longer be valid. The views expressed in this work are solely those of the author and do not necessarily reflect the views of the publisher, and the publisher hereby disclaims any responsibility for them.

Any people depicted in stock imagery provided by Thinkstock are models, and such images are being used for illustrative purposes only. Certain stock imagery © Thinkstock.

ISBN: 978-1-5127-7444-3 (sc)
ISBN: 978-1-5127-7443-6 (e)

Library of Congress Control Number: 2017901825

Print information available on the last page.

WestBow Press rev. date: 04/07/2017

to the next generation of believers—
Lukas, Olivia, Avery, Noelle, and Logan...

CONTENTS

INTRODUCTION—ENJOY

We are so excited for you to come along with us on this journey. We will taste some good food, hear some good stories, cry a little, laugh a lot, and be completely amazed at what God reveals. We will see how the essence of food defines the very nature of God, his presence, and his love. We will also see how food's narrative exposes a sinister plot—an evil effort to tempt and deceive us. Nevertheless, our response to one extraordinary meal invitation will lead us to a banquet of unparalleled excellence, experience, satisfaction, and joy.

While this is not a diet guide or a meal planner, each chapter highlights a food type and its unique characteristics. Most important, you will see how God personally interacts with us from the garden to the table. Each relationship-based segment begins with an intro question that will help you to engage with the topics, and concludes with a fun and personal (everything but the) Kitchen Sink exercise.

Chapters end with suggested dishes to prepare and share as a group. This part of the lesson will not only be enjoyable, but insightful as well. Participation will heighten your culinary senses, relate to your experience, and make memorable and useful the lesson topics. For more information, please see the Group Taste-and-See Experience Guidelines.

Twenty-five lessons and five Group Taste-and-See Experience opportunities explore God's presence and his desire to be known in every aspect of our dining experience. Choose to complete one to five lessons per week—depending your group's study patterns and/or time parameters. Please refer to the Scheduling Options Chart to select a class schedule that fits your needs.

Our original intent for this study was to provide practical help for preparing meals, and to introduce God's Word through the familiar experience of serving food. However, while writing these lessons, we discovered something completely unexpected—we discovered how beautifully the Gospel presents itself through the intimate language of food. The Gospel is easy, and wonderful, and powerful, and full of mercy and grace. The Gospel is for everyone. So come along with us. "Taste and see that the LORD is good" (Psalm 34:8 NIV).

We sincerely pray you enjoy—bon appétit.

Londie and Kriss

And God saw every thing that he had made,
and, behold, it was very good.
—Genesis 1:31 (KJV)

THE GIFT

- Objective: Discover how the packaging of food tells a relationship story with emotional and spiritual implications.
- Bible Topic: Truth and deception relate to what we are hungering for.
- Meal Topic: The presentation of food engages our senses and evokes a response.
- Food Topic: Fruit
- Food To Be Prepared: Jam, Salsa, or Pesto

PART 1: INTRO QUESTION

Let us begin with a personal question to whet your appetite.

 What is your favorite childhood food memory?

What is it about a food memory that is so endearing? What links emotions to a bite of food? If you took the time to ponder the intro question, you may have experienced a sense of joy or a moment of escape. Your memory may have been of a rare meal at your grandmother's house, or perhaps you recalled an old neighborhood where school friends invited you to dinner. Memories like these are little gifts, packaged and set aside in your past.

As we begin our study, consider the intimate nature of food. Each bite is uniquely yours to experience. Each meal includes a story—your story. Each story reveals a relationship.

ENJOY! IT'S A GIFT

Our study begins in the garden of Eden. Imagine being there and suddenly being alive. Let us explore this ideal setting to discover what preparations set the stage for the first food memory and the first conversations about food.

Please read Genesis 2:4–15.

 What do these verses say about the nature of garden fruit? (v. 9)

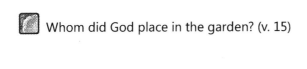 Whom did God place in the garden? (v. 15)

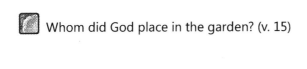 What two trees, planted in the middle of the garden, became center focus in the story? (v. 9)

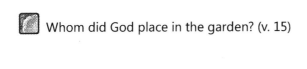 Who planted the garden? (v. 8)

Do you wonder who this God is? Have you ever thought about who brightened the night landscape with stars? Do you know him, the one who designed every stone, in every color, and who created the vast terrain of the earth for giraffes and hummingbirds? He is the one who planted a garden and created a venue for the first food memory of humankind. He is the one who first spoke about food.

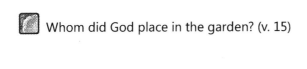 Please read Genesis 1:26–31. The first recorded food memory recalls a conversation with God. From these verses, what did God say about food?

Then God said, "I give you ... food."
—Genesis 1:29 (NIV)

Please continue to read Genesis 2:15–25. What was important for Adam to remember about eating from the trees in the garden? (vv. 16–17)

Was Adam free to eat from the tree of life?

The garden's design provided more than something to eat and a beautiful venue to experience—it gave Adam something to do. The garden provided the opportunity to enjoy work and to perceive that the effort was good.

Please complete the verse below, Ecclesiastes 3:13 (KJV).

> And also that every man should eat and drink,
> and enjoy the good of all his labour,
> it *is* the _____ of God.

What became Adam's role in the garden? (Genesis 2:5, 15)

For a Bit More to Chew On: Consider what benefits the garden experience might provide. Beyond food, what benefits come from working in a garden?

Have you ever wondered what the garden in Eden looked like? Were the trees in groves, perfectly manicured, or were they wild and a little random? Were trees lined up two-by-two in a heavenly alphabetical order or by variety—citrus here, tropical there? Did Adam get around to tasting every fruit? Did Eve have a favorite? As they tended the garden, they experienced everything from exercise and opportunity to the reward of creativity. However, it is also interesting to consider that God chose the beauty of a fruit tree to describe creation.

The way fruit is packaged is clearly important in the dialogue. Consider the first dinner, the first meal. Consider the display. It was a colorful buffet gracefully surrounded by lively leaves and branches. The textures were different, the flavors were unknown, and the scents were inviting. Additionally, the fruit was attractive and intended for visual pleasure.

To enhance your understanding of God's attention to detail and design, please describe what you see when looking at fruit. What is it about fruit that is delightful to see?

Personal Observation: What is your garden experience? In light of these few verses, what does a piece of fruit tell you about God and his relationship with you?

Perhaps you have never considered the first garden meal as a source of inspiration for your dining room, or maybe you have never seen fruit as a delightful layering of nourishment, enjoyment, provision, and purpose all wrapped in a decorated package. The next time you browse through the produce section of the grocery store or have the occasion to shop a farmer's market, imagine the fruit hanging on a tree, in a garden, pleasing to the sight; imagine the fruit as little reminders of creation—as God's gift to you.

Thanks be to God for his indescribable gift!
—2 Corinthians 9:15 (NIV)

THE KITCHEN SINK—PACKAGING

We can only imagine that Eden's garden was splendid, with the presentation of fruits and vegetables being abundant and inviting. Unable to harvest every fruit in a single day, Adam and Eve were able to select what drew their attention, perhaps what was nearby. They discovered the bounty as they pleased.

To discover your own culinary pursuit or shopping style, browse through your pantry or refrigerator and identify several food items that you have personally selected to eat. List these items in the first column on the chart below. Then mark one or more categories that influenced your decision to choose this food item. Afterward, note your observations.

Food Item	Price	Package or Marketing Influence	Nutrition	Location of Purchase	Calories	Taste or Flavor	Convenience

How did the packaging or presentation influence your product decisions?

Part 2: Intro Question

When you think of a gift, it is probably not something hanging from a tree. So ...

What would a perfectly wrapped gift look like to you? Use your imagination and explore the synapses in your brain to describe a gorgeous, beautifully wrapped package; include its colors, patterns, and layers of interest. Also include what you hope is inside.

Gifts come in all sizes and shapes, but sometimes the packaging, the outward appearance, or the presentation deceives us. The first deception of humankind had to do with the repackaging of a gift. Today we will see, from the third chapter in Genesis, how the serpent subtly rewrapped the beauty of fruit; then he used a powerful marketing pitch and sold it to Eve as something more to be desired—readily available and just over there—hanging from a tree.

Do Not Open

Please read Genesis 3:1–24.

Which tree was the topic of conversation between Eve and the serpent?

What question did the serpent ask that led Eve to focus on a particular tree?

In her conversation with the serpent, how did Eve explain God's command? (Genesis 3:3b)
Eve said that God said, _____

_____.

On which tree did the enticing and dangerous fruit grow? (Also read Genesis 2:17)

Fruit from the tree in the middle of the garden provided knowledge, but knowledge of what? Please take a minute to consider, from the original Hebrew words, the meaning of *good* and *evil*.

On the list below, highlight or underline specific terms that stand out to you. Consider all that *worst* implies.

Strong's **Hebrew Definition for #2896**	*Strong's* **Hebrew Definition for # 7451**
(*good*) // bwj // towb // tobe //	(*evil*) // er // ra` // rah //
adj.	**adj.**
good, pleasant, agreeable	bad, evil
pleasant, agreeable (to the senses)	bad, disagreeable, malignant
pleasant (to the higher nature)	bad, unpleasant, evil (giving pain,
good, excellent (of its kind)	unhappiness, misery)
good, rich, valuable in estimation	evil, displeasing
good, appropriate, becoming	bad (of its kind – land, water, etc.)
better (comparative)	bad (of value)
glad, happy, prosperous (of man's sensuous	worse than, worst (comparison)
nature)	sad, unhappy
good understanding (of man's intellectual	evil (hurtful)
nature)	bad, unkind (vicious in disposition)
good, kind, benign	bad, evil, wicked (ethically)
good, right (ethical)	in general, of persons, of thoughts
	deeds, actions
noun	
a good thing, benefit, welfare	**noun**
welfare, prosperity, happiness	evil, distress, misery, injury, calamity
good things (collective)	evil, distress, adversity
good, benefit	evil, injury, wrong
moral good	evil (ethical)
welfare, benefit, good things	evil, misery, distress, injury
welfare, prosperity, happiness	evil, misery, distress
good things (collective)	evil, injury, wrong
bounty	evil (ethical)

—*Strong's Exhaustive Concordance of the Bible*

The words *good* and *evil* show a contrast; they are tangibly opposite. If you read about the six days of creation in Genesis, you will notice that at the end of each day, God saw that what he had made was *good.*

What did God conclude at the end of all creation? Please write the first sentence of Genesis 1:31.

The same Hebrew word for *good* used to describe creation in Genesis 1:31 is also used to identify the tree of the knowledge of good and evil.

By inference, can we assume that Adam and Eve had the knowledge of good, but not by contrast? Adam and Eve were experiencing only good, since everything that God created was *very good.* They had not yet the knowledge of the opposite, that which is evil, because they had not experienced bad, unpleasantness, displeasure, worse than, worst, sadness, or even unhappiness.

Please read again Genesis 3:4–5. How did the serpent market the fruit to the woman? What did he say about eating fruit from the tree in the middle of the garden?

Genesis 3:6 describes how Eve's perception changed. Was the serpent's lie believable? How did she view the fruit after listening to the serpent?

What were the first glimpses of evil for Adam and Eve? What did they come to know? What became unpleasant for them? (Genesis 3:7–10)

Imagine a package, attractively wrapped and topped with a shimmery satin bow. The lid on the package, wrapped separately, sides off easily. Once opened, an incredible force propels you into unfamiliar realm. The power of its content is indescribable; it is something you have never experienced and something you never desired. You instantly know why there was a warning on the label; you instantly understand your first compulsion to run. However, because you did not resist, you come to know what is in the package—and within the irresistible wrappings comes the knowledge of evil.

Adam and Eve chose to eat from the tree in the middle of the garden. The verses that follow (Genesis 3:11–24) describe the consequence of Eve's gullible, trusting temperament and Adam's sin. They did not *physically* die instantaneously—as one might suppose from the warning. However, something very important was removed from their grasp.

Please read again Genesis 3:22–24.

Which tree was now guarded by Cherubim and why? (Genesis 3:22–24)

What benefit comes from eating fruit from the tree of life? (v. 22)

The first deception story had to do with food. A few well-crafted words manipulated Eve and enticed her to hunger for and desire wisdom. One might presume that wisdom is good and worth the risk of disobedience. Certainly, the appetite for wisdom should come with reward. However, Eve's path to wisdom led her astray. She followed the wrong voice.

Is it possible that what Eve desired was already available to her? According to James 1:5, what is the recipe for finding wisdom?

Please write James 1:5.

Instead of asking God for wisdom, Eve was deceived into accepting a counterfeit package—she exchanged God's protection for a lie. The fruit on each garden tree was wrapped in engaging colors and textures, with interesting shapes and sizes. Every fruit was pleasing to the sight—fragrant and good for food. The serpent used his words to repackage and present an *even better* choice. He offered food for the intellect—an intriguing offer. With this choice came the knowledge of evil.

Adam became afraid with the knowledge of evil, and a sentence of death followed his fear. Do you suppose death came because God never wanted people to live forever with the experience of evil? Did mercy banish Adam and Eve from the garden and the tree of life?

You may be wondering what this story in the garden has to do with cooking today or getting a meal on the table. Well, basically—everything. We can learn from these few verses how food's design reveals God's creation, his provision, his love for us, his sovereignty, and his plans for good. With each meal, with each taste, comes a reminder of his presence. The story also exposes tactics and maneuvers designed to hijack the gift—subtle lures to distract and deceive us from the experience of food's intended delight. God's packaging is expressive, and his presentation is with purpose—a gift from him to enjoy.

The question remains, what are you hungering for?

Blessed are those who hunger and thirst for righteousness,
for they will be filled.
—Matthew 5:6 (NIV)

THE KITCHEN SINK—THE TASTE OF WORDS

In this lesson, we saw that words are a form of packaging and presentation. What we say about food is relevant to the experience. How we say it is also impactful.

Enjoy a minute or so of pretend time. As a practice presentation, describe a favorite salsa, pesto, or jam—recipes from the garden. Remember, creativity is part of who you are—it's in your DNA. Please include how this dish might look and taste. Briefly note how you might serve it and what memories might be made.

PART 3: INTRO QUESTION

 How would you describe the best food gift that you have ever received? Also, please note the giver's attitude.

Since God is the Creator and we are created in his image (Genesis 1:27), it is no wonder that we too want to be creative. We have also touched on the fact that God gives gifts. Today, we will see that God also accepts gifts. It would follow that—because we are created in his image—we too have a propensity to give and receive gifts. Consider how our attitudes are reflected in the gifts we give. Consider how our attitudes influence the way our gifts are received.

FOOD FIGHT

God gave the first gift mentioned in the Bible. It was the free and plentiful supply of good food, first given to Adam and then extended to all living creatures and humanity. Interestingly, the next gifts mentioned were also food. These gifts—given to God—tell us something further about relationships.

The characters in today's lesson are brothers, the sons of Adam and Eve. The story takes place outside of Eden, in a field.

Please read Genesis 4:1–16

Compare the description of the two gifts. (vv. 3–4)

What was the result of Abel's offering?

What was the result of Cain's offering?

Genesis 4:1–16 reads like a synopsis for a bestselling suspense novel, a TV miniseries, or a Broadway musical. This brief narrative about Cain and Able even includes stage cues for the actor's demeanor, expression, and posture.

Please reread Genesis 4:3–8.

The King James Version reads, "And Cain was very wroth, and his countenance fell" (Genesis 4:5b). Please look up and define the word *countenance*.

Have you ever served a meal that was not accepted? Did your countenance fall? Was your expression an obvious clue to the way you felt? Please identify reasons for your meal's rejection, even if it was not your fault.

Can you relate to Cain's feelings based on your experience with an unappreciated meal? Please briefly explain.

Cain became very angry because his gift was not accepted. It was visibly and physically apparent that he was troubled and extremely angry. Please review the definition of *anger*, from the original Hebrew text. Underline words that you may have experienced with intense emotion.

Strong's Hebrew Definition for # 02734
(wroth, angry) // hrx // charah // khaw–raw'//
to be hot, furious, burn, become angry, be kindled
(Qal) to burn, kindle (anger)
(Niphal) to be angry with, be incensed
(Hiphil) to burn, kindle

Then the LORD said to Cain, "*Why are you angry?* Why is your face downcast?"
—Genesis 4:6 (NIV, emphasis added)

God followed these questions with a rebuke and a warning. What does the Genesis 4:7b tell us about sin? Please write it in your own words.

What was the result of Cain's anger?

Cain did not heed God's warning about sin's desire for him. He did not exercise dominion over it. He did not conquer the temptation to vindicate himself. Through the power of his own hands—yielding to the tormenting words and feelings in his mind and heart—Cain killed his younger brother over a gift of food.

 What questions come to mind as you read this story?

These verses are hard to understand. Perhaps you just had to be there. The conversation about why Cain's gift was not accepted is broad and haunting. Was his fruit a less valuable commodity than a lamb? Yet God made the fruit; he called it good and gave it to man. Was the offense an issue of re-gifting? Was it Cain's attitude? One might think, *What does God need, anyway?* Was God going to eat the fruit? Certainly, the best fruit should be saved for a hungry child. Moreover, how is killing a lamb better, or was the sacrifice necessary? Was there a mysterious and spiritual foreshadowing in the sacrifice of a lamb? It might be that Able's gift was *more excellent* because he offered it by faith. Does that mean that Cain's was not?

Not one part of this story is without purpose and instruction. Scholars will continue to search for the dialogue to explain this mystery. What we do know, however, is this:

 Please write Hebrews 11:4a.

According to the original Greek translation, faith is "the conviction that God exists and is the creator and ruler of all things ..." (*Strong's*, pistis, #4102). Able brought his gift to the one he knew to be the creator of the universe and the ruler of all things. It was a gift offered as an expression of honor. Do you wonder what Cain was thinking?

By faith Abel offered unto God a more excellent sacrifice than Cain ...
—Hebrews 11:4a (KJV)

Please read Hebrews 11:1–6

 What is necessary to please God? (Hebrews 11:6)

 What further impact did Cain's anger bring to his family? Consider Genesis 4:14.

We see that the first two tragedies in the Bible include relationships with God and stories about food. In both cases, a counterfeit truth led to death. Distress, misery, injury, and calamity became a new form of evil for Adam and Eve to know. The death of their son was an even greater contrast to the *only good* that Adam and Eve once experienced.

 How did Cain's anger over a gift of food affect his relationship with God? (Genesis 4:16)

Personal Observation:

In the dramatic account of Cain and Able, evil becomes the contrast that magnifies the goodness of God's plan for us. We have and experience—because of Adam and Eve—the knowledge of good and evil. Even so, no amount of evil can diminish the goodness that God created. In the same way that light will always push back darkness and the flame of a candle will always light a room, good overcomes evil. We will continue to study and see how food reveals this very good and delicious part of the story.

Thou wilt shew me the path of life:
in thy presence is fulness of joy;
at thy right hand there are pleasures for evermore.
—Psalm 16:11 (KJV)

THE KITCHEN SINK—A PLEASANT SOUND

In the last lesson, you wrote a description for salsa, pesto, or jam. Now let us take it a step further and write a simple menu that is pleasing to hear. The purpose of this exercise is to experience how menus communicate emotion with words about food.

First, compare these two dinner menu renditions.

Dinner is cheeseburgers, French fries, and corn on the cob.

or

Tonight we will be eating fresh-ground sirloin patties, seasoned with garlic salt and pepper—topped with crumbled blue cheese, lettuce, and pickles— served on toasted oat buns. They are accompanied by julienne potatoes— oven-fried with olive oil and minced garlic—and market-fresh corn.

Imagine viewing your grocery cart or writing your grocery list for these meals. Do you see a difference based on the two descriptions? Do the dishes somehow look different to you? Do they sound different?

 For practice, embellish and market this straightforward menu.

Grilled cheese sandwich, tomato soup, and iced tea.

Feel free to substitute if you are lactose intolerant or do not like tomato soup. After all, it is your kitchen. Listed on the next page are a few foodie terms—to assist your *more excellent* effort.

Seasonings: cayenne, garlic, onion salt, oregano, parsley, paprika, turmeric, butter, margarine, olive oil

Cooking Terms: bubbling, grilled, sautéed, toasted, baked, pan-fried, roasted, healthy, creamy, caramelized, stuffed

Garnishes: pickles, tomatoes, parsley, olives, capers, pickled ginger, horseradish, rosemary, basil, cilantro

Types of Cheese: pepper jack, cheddar, Swiss, blue cheese, asiago, provolone, parmesan, gorgonzola

Types of Bread: marbled rye, sour dough, French, Rainbow, whole wheat, wheat berry, potato bread, ciabatta, pita, focaccia, gluten-free

Beverage Terms: infused with, cold-brewed, steeped, chilled, iced, tangy, rich, full-bodied, mellow, over-the-top

Other Terms: fresh, garden-grown, homegrown, imported, seasonal, juicy, firm, ripe, tasty, delicious, mouthwatering

PART 4: INTRO QUESTION

 Has a philosophy of food ever presented you with a source of difficulty or troublesome expectation? How does that message influence you today?

It would be great if we could write a study about the glories and wonders of the garden of Eden and miraculously enable you to prepare healthy, fabulous, and delicious meals, every day. However, while a study of the luscious garden may inspire you to do so, it might not equip you for the challenge.

There is a challenge, and the challenge comes in many forms. In part, the challenge has intensified with modern conveniences; in part, it has intensified as society overwhelms us with choice, distractions, and alternatives. We need to realize that beneath the glamour and hype of advertisement, and beneath the quick-and-easy packaging, there may lie a snare. Behind the frozen, ready-made substitutes and the guilt-laden, "ten easy ways to do anything" articles lurks that same nemesis of old: the devil, the serpent, the more subtle than any beast of the field—snake in the grass.

ANOTHER GARDEN TALE

Satan, the author of confusion and the father of lies, plays havoc in the garden and he plays havoc in the kitchen. We can learn to rise above his tactics, but we should not ignore them. In fact, we should be keenly aware of them. Today's lesson, taught in parables, identifies the enemy's distracting maneuvers and destructive schemes while the food for our table is still in the field.

 Please use a dictionary and write the definition of *enemy*.

Please read Matthew 13:24–30. Keep the definition of enemy in mind as you read the parable, as told by Jesus.

Who planted the good seed?

 Tares, a term used in the King James Version, are a kind of weed, resembling wheat, except the grains are black. Who planted the tares/ weeds? (v. 25)

 Based on your understanding of gardening or farming, why would an enemy plant weeds in a farmer's field? What might be his motivation?

 Jesus relates this parable to a kingdom he knows well. Whose kingdom is it? (v. 24)

Please read Matthew 13:36–43.

 Note how Jesus explains the parable.

- ○ Who planted the tares or weeds?

- ○ Who is the enemy?

- ○ Who are the tares/weeds?

- ○ Who are the good seed?

- ○ Who planted the good seed?

 Where are the tares and the good seed planted? (v. 38)

Jesus explains that the kingdom of heaven is like a farmer's field where wheat and weeds are planted; side-by-side they grow and live together. There is a purpose, of course, for each crop. The wheat will produce fruit—food for harvest. The weeds and tares yield thorns and produce a crop that offends.

Personal Insight:

In a similar parable, Jesus identifies the consequence of thorns. Please read Mark 4:1–9.

What happened to the seed that fell among thorns? (Mark 4:7)

What happened to the seed sown on good soil? (Mark 4:8)

Please continue to read Mark 4:10–20. Jesus once again identifies the characters in the story.

What type of seed does the farmer plant in this parable? (Mark 4:14)

What are the enemy's tactics? (Mark 4:15–19)

How does Jesus identify good soil in Mark 4:20?

We might think of an enemy as one who engages in conflicts during war, in business, or perhaps in relationships. The battles are over ideals, property, or power. Strength and an undeniable presence are his advantage. A thief, on the other hand, prefers no conflict. A thief, in fact, hopes to take what he wants and plans to escape unnoticed. Consider what he is looking for. He too is looking for something of value.

What is the warning in 1 Peter 5:8?

If the enemy is the devil, what is it he is trying to steal? If he is stealing the seed, what crop is he trying to prevent? If the seed is the Word of God, what is the fruit?

 Please read Galatians 5:22–23. From these verses, describe good fruit.

Do you remember this verse? Please fill in the blanks (Ecclesiastes 3:13 KJV).

And also that every man should eat and drink,

and _____ of all his _____,

it *is* the _____ of God.

Food from the garden is a daily reminder of God's presence, his gift, and his purpose for us. If the enemy can effectively change our focus, repackage the garden, and blur the view with weeds and thorns, there is a possibility that he plans to rob our joy—the *enjoy* of life.

Perhaps you are familiar with the phrase coined by President Harry Truman, "If you can't stand the heat, get out of the kitchen." Of course, he was referring to troublesome events brought on by political enemies, but the reference to the kitchen is telling. Many have yielded to that battle cry, waved the white flag, and given up precious ground in their own homes. They have surrendered their joy.

It is time to replenish the fruit bowls!

 What is the hope of the one who plants the seed in Mark 4:20b?

I planted the seed, Apollos watered it, but God made it grow.
—1 Corinthians 3:6 (NIV)

THE KITCHEN SINK—FACE THE FACTS

In the same way that we can identify an apple or pear by its appearance, it is possible to recognize spiritual fruit by the look on our faces. Place one or several mirrors in easy view around you kitchen. As you do chores, prepare a meal, or even just have a conversation, check your countenance now and again. A glance into the mirror—to view the look on your face—may reveal some unexpected harvest.

Please record your findings.

- ☐ The joy on my face was extraordinary.
- ☐ I am happy to report I was smiling.
- ☐ I saw no smile—but no frown.
- ☐ There was a slight grimace.
- ☐ The weeds in my garden have completely taken over. I need the master gardener's help.

PART 5: INTRO QUESTION

[image] What question or insight caught your attention and touched your heart in The Gift chapter? Was it a food memory, the discussion about gifts, or a Kitchen Sink exercise? Was it a still-small voice? Briefly explain.

Our heart is a little like a food pantry. Occasionally, a deep cleaning is in order. From time to time, we discover new recipes, and we stock up on fresh and perhaps unexpected ingredients. Certainly, the meals we serve are a reflection of what we have gathered.

God sees our heart in the kitchen. He sees the thankful and generous heart. He also sees the broken-hearted, the heavy-laden, the uninspired, the tired, and the very tired. However, beyond a grocery list, he has a recipe—and it is not something to measure with a spoon. It is a recipe for an abundant life.

I WANT THAT RECIPE

In this lesson, we will continue to look at how food is packaged and presented. We will also see how it relates to an abundant life. First, let us get an idea of what that means.

[image] Please read the words of Jesus in John 10:10. What type of life did Jesus come to give?

The phrase in John 10:10 "more abundantly" (KJV) or "have it to the full" (NIV) is translated from the Greek word *perissos* (*Strong's*, #4053)—meaning "superior, extraordinary, uncommon, and more remarkable." Consider the flavor of his recipe—a superior, extraordinary, uncommon, and more remarkable life.

[image] Since we are talking about the packaging and presentation of food, what might an uncommon, extraordinary, and more remarkable dining experience look like? Think grand and write a few things down.

Did your extraordinary meal idea include chandeliers or a brilliant sunset? Were appetizers served in a hot air balloon, with food prepared exactly the way you like it? On the other hand, did you think *extraordinary*, in the miraculous sense? Did it challenge the traditional? Did it make you pause?

When you think about it, there is nothing normal about the extraordinary. The extraordinary shows up when the expected has failed to arrive, when the parameters of traditional are stretched. The extraordinary is not served carefully, with naive ideals, but it is splendid by God's design. Today's Bible stories include several meals that were prepared and presented in an unexpected and remarkable fashion. They offer a peek into the menu of a more abundant life.

We can more appreciate these stories with little information about the main character, Elijah; he is first mentioned in 1 Kings 17. As his story evolves, we find that Elijah is a prophet, and his continual focus is to challenge the status quo of a wayward Israel. He set out to make his God known, living his life to the fullest in a less than idyllic setting. Elijah's meals fall into the extraordinary category. The story begins when Elijah confronts Ahab, the very wicked king of Israel.

Please read 1 Kings 17:1–9.

 What did Elijah announce to Ahab, in verse 1?

To proclaim a drought for several years and to announce that there would not even be dew on the ground, in any generation, is severe. Of course, a drought would most directly affect the food supply. Eventually, water supplies would be inadequate to sustain a nation. It was a judgment call—Ahab's ways were not acceptable.

Concerning Ahab, please recall the definition of *evil*: worse than, worst, distress, misery, injury, and calamity. The same Hebrew word for *evil* that identifies the tree of the knowledge of good and evil also describes Ahab.

To better understand Ahab's character, please read 1 Kings 16:30–33.

These verses describe Ahab as more (what)?

Ahab did more evil in the eyes of the LORD than any of those before him. With your personal knowledge of evil rulers in history, consider what terrible things might have taken place under his reign. Then think worse than that. It was for these reasons that a drought ensued—it was a harsh judgment. Yet, by contrast, it was because of this evil that we get another glimpse of God and a glimpse of some very extraordinary meals.

Please read again 1 Kings 17:1–9.

 How did God communicate his menu to Elijah? (v. 2)

 Who delivered Elijah's food? (v. 4)

 What was the menu? (v. 6)

Even on the surface, this is quite a tale. If we dip our toes in the cool brook and find a comfortable rock to sit on, what else do we come to know? Elijah was hiding from a most evil king. He was also isolated from the people in his kingdom for a very long time. Hiding near a brook, he somehow concealed himself from obvious view. The babble of the brook and the vast cloudless sky became a backdrop for his breakfast in the morning and his dinner at night. Each day, he waited, and each day, they came—ravens delivering his food. He drank from the brook, and each day there was no rain.

As time passed, patience patterned Elijah's existence. With each meal came the evidence of his God. With each day came another meal—with ravens for companionship. With each meal came bread—baked somewhere else. With each day came one more day away from normal life. Then one day the word of the Lord came to Elijah—it was time to get up and move.

Please read 1 Kings 17:8–24 to see what happened next.

What do you find uncommon and remarkable about the meals served in these verses?

Please read again 1 Kings 17:24.

What evidence of God's presence with Elijah followed these meals? (vv. 17–23)

Miracles surrounded the life of Elijah. Yet Elijah was a man, and for anyone, an abundant life does not come without trials. In spite of his remarkable experiences, Elijah still had fears and despair. He still needed comfort and reassurance in times of distress and anxiety. When Jezebel, the wife of Ahab, sought to kill Elijah, he was afraid and fled to the wilderness. Once again, the Lord prepared food to comfort him.

Please read 1 Kings 19:1–13.

How did God's assurance and hope come to Elijah after these miraculous meals? (1 Kings 19:12)

Personal Insight:

Elijah was a man of great faith. He had many opportunities to prove that the Word of God was true in his life. He lived an extraordinary life and enjoyed extraordinary meals.

Do these stories add to your previous concept of an extraordinary meal? An abundant life—superior and extraordinary—is the supernatural evidence of God.

Yet there is a thief. He prefers that we abandon the truth to settle for a decidedly inferior product. His lies are many, and deliberate, and subtle—adding fear and anxiety. As we embrace God's gift, he will try to steal our joy. But, good news— the Son of God came to destroy the devil's work. Jesus came with a plan, and it is really quite delicious.

Please write 1 John 3:8b.

O taste and see that the LORD is good.
—Psalm 34:8a (KJV)

THE KITCHEN SINK—FIND AMAZING

It is our hope that at the end of each chapter, you will enjoy a group discussion centered around the chapter's food topic—in this case, fruit. The next page includes details for your group experience opportunity.

For today, briefly note the types of enjoyment that you have experienced during mealtime this week. How have you enjoyed the gift of God?

Please review the next page to prepare for the Group Taste-and-See Experience.

Group Taste-and-See Experience

GARDEN FAVORITES: PESTO, SALSA, JAM

With the garden in mind, please choose one of the three condiment suggestions to prepare and share with your study group: pesto, salsa, or jam. Use packaged, fresh, or epicurean recipes—choose recipes according to your taste, budget, and available time. Bring samples of the ingredients used to prepare your dish. Each group member will display their ingredients and present them for sampling and discussion during the Group Taste-and-See Experience. For additional insight, discuss how the packaging influenced your purchase—display the cans and ready-mix packages for observation. Also, include a sample of the packaged products for taste and visual comparisons.

Before you begin, please read the **Group Taste-and-See Experience Guidelines** (in the back of the book). As a group, you will decide how this part of the lesson will develop and determine the participation plan. If you are studying alone, invite someone to join you for this exercise. Below are discussion suggestions for this chapter's Group Taste-and-See Experience.

DISCUSSION SUGGESTIONS

Remember, presentation is important—include smiles. Please be respectful of each opinion and graceful in your conversation, especially if there are timid cooks amongst you.

- Compare canned products to fresh produce or dried versions. Compare the flavors, colors, textures, and cost.
- Discuss the time involved for shopping and preparation for each version.
- Discuss the cost of various versions—canned, fresh, and epicurean.
- Compare the overall appearance and enjoyment of each sample.
- Discuss new insights about God's gift of food with its relationship to packaging and presentation.
- Discuss how you see God's presence in the presentation of food.

Mealtimes engage each of us in different and unique ways. Most meal plans employ a daily routine. However, some meals have an eternal purpose. In this chapter, we will embrace the meal preparations and the entire event. Preparations include our heart, the food, and the setting. We will see how God's plan includes you and his glory.

For I know the plans I have for you, declares the LORD.
—Jeremiah 29:11a (NIV)

THE PLAN

- Objective: View meals as events with eternal importance.
- Bible Topic: The wilderness is a place with purpose.
- Meal Topic: The venue is the setting for a celebration to remember.
- Food Topic: Spices and Herbs
- Food to be Prepared: Sauces and Dips

PART 1: INTRO QUESTION

When attending a planned dining event, what part of the meal do you most enjoy?

When you consider the planning that goes in to a wedding banquet, a holiday reunion, or even a special birthday party, you realize that part of the plan includes the venue—the place or location of the event. The venue layers expression into an event. It expresses the significance and mood of the occasion, and it remains an integral part of the memory. We often recall these types of occasions based on how well we were treated, how comfortable we were, or how quickly we wanted to leave. As we examine several significant meal events, begin to translate elements of these planned venues to your own dining room or kitchen. Consider how they relate to the people at your table and the memories that they create—perhaps for generations, possibly forever.

DINNER WITH A VIEW

The first venue we will explore is a room prepared for a very famous celebration meal. Because this location has a well-known history, it is easy to rehearse the story in our minds without considering the details or the planning that took place ahead of time. The celebration was Passover: an annual event, a centuries-old Jewish tradition. The setting included the atmosphere for the meal famously known as the *Last Supper*.

It is important to know that the evening of the very first Passover included the preparation of a meal. The menu was specific: a roasted lamb with bitter herbs and bread without yeast—that is, unleavened bread. All of the items on the menu held a significant meaning, and they were required for the meal.

Please read Luke 22:7–23.

From the brief description in Luke 22:7–23, imagine the venue for this meal. Please take a moment to describe the details that were most likely included in the preparations. Gather your clues from the text.

Jesus was planning to observe Passover, and he needed a venue—a secure location to gather with his disciples. The arrangement included a secluded guest room— sheltered from view—a table, and food to prepare. However, the setting pulsed beyond those upper room walls; preparations for the feast occupied all of Jerusalem. Because of the celebration, the city was overflowing with visiting Jews and their families. Similar to any major modern-day event, merchants sought an easy profit, security heightened, and politicians looked for every opportunity to advance their agenda. Jesus had reached celebrity status; the many miracles he had performed and the fame of his teachings created excitement everywhere he went. The external atmosphere was undoubtedly present in the hearts and minds of those he invited to this very private venue.

As you read the following narratives, imagine being a part of this entourage and traveling with Jesus to Jerusalem. The first narrative begins as Jesus raises Lazarus from the dead.

John 11:43–57 details the broad reaction to Jesus and his presence shortly after he raised Lazarus from the grave. Please read this account and complete the following observation. (v. 45)

Many Jews _____.

Why were the chief priests and Pharisees concerned? (v. 48)

Why did Jesus begin to avoid the crowds? (vv. 53–54)

How did the chief priests and Pharisees respond? (v. 57)

For a Bit More to Chew On: From your own experience, consider the activity and energy of a very large crowd that centrally gathers for a major event. Briefly describe what that energy and focus might look like without the constraints of bleachers, stadium walls, parking lots, or cell phones.

With this in mind, consider the streets of Jerusalem days before Passover. To continue with the backdrop for this setting, please also read John 12:1–19.

 What observation did the Pharisees make six days before Passover? (John 12:11, 19)

Imagine the sounds of the crowd in the distance. Imagine how his disciples felt being a part of something so big, so spectacular, and so prophetic. Imagine the clandestine whispers as the plot to betray Jesus wove its way through the crowd.

Jesus was preparing to share the most intimate meal of his life with his dearest friends. This Passover meal—planned to be private, by invitation only—provided a backdrop for an eternal purpose. Jesus knew the impact of this meal would affect every nation, for eternity. The agenda had scripted and prophetic foreshadowing, and everything would be documented. The throngs of people that followed and sought Jesus presented a huge challenge for privacy and security. The venue had to be perfect—not happenstance, not arbitrary.

 What did Jesus instruct Peter and John to do, concerning the venue? (Luke 22:8–12)

Peter knew that everywhere Jesus went, the unexpected happened. John witnessed the exceptional love and compassion of Jesus. Nevertheless, had he come to believe that all things were possible?

Think for a moment about the guarded details and measures that were necessary for the success of this meal. Had Jesus pulled you aside and said, "I need you to take care of this for me," how would you have responded? Would you have prayed over each utensil and polished every chair?

When it was time to eat, what emotion did Jesus express? What words stand out to you? (Luke 22:15)

If you are new to the study of the Last Supper, sit back and embrace the view that the twelve disciples shared. Realize that the planning included a specific menu, setting, and atmosphere. The large upper room was prepared to accommodate all that would take place; a group of men gathered to witness the moment in time—a meal that divided the centuries. The significance of the meal was unknown to everyone—except, of course, to Jesus. Even Judas had no idea that he was participating in the master's plan—a plan that included a dish and a dipped piece of bread (John 13:18–30). The plan also included an opportunity to believe.

And he said to them, "I have eagerly desired to eat this Passover
with you before I suffer."
—Luke 22:15 (NIV)

THE KITCHEN SINK—EAGER DESIRES

Jesus eagerly desired to eat the Passover with his disciples. Meticulous plans were involved in order to set the stage for the fulfillment of his desire. How might we learn from this as our dreams and hopes lie before us—as we gather friends or family around the table?

Identify the thought pattern that goes through your mind when preparing a room for your family meal or for a meal with guests.

Now, intentionally, rewrite your description and edit the pattern to include a desire of your heart.

What is your prayer?

PART 2: INTRO QUESTION

Sometimes our schedule or itinerary calls for a quick meal or a meal on the go. Even these meals require a plan.

 What was your most memorable meal on the go? Briefly describe.

PLANS FOR DINNER

Today's meal event takes place in a remote and unfamiliar venue, in the homes of Egyptian slaves. It was their last meal before their journey to the Promised Land began. While our focus will be on the venue and the atmosphere, a little background information about the people will help.

Dwelling in Goshen, the best land of Egypt, the children of Israel had become a mighty people, and Egypt's Pharaoh feared their numbers. In an effort to control them, Pharaoh forced God's people into slavery. Because of their growing population, Pharaoh ordered midwives to kill the baby boys at birth. When this attempt failed, he ordered the people to cast newborn sons into the river.

As an infant, Moses escaped this mass execution attempt and harsh existence when Pharaoh's daughter rescued him from the Nile and raised him as her own. As time passed, Moses struggled with conflicting loyalty between his people and his regal home with Pharaoh, so he fled Egypt. After forty years, however, Moses returned. He returned to the Egyptian palace with a message from God—"Let my people go."

Our story begins after a series of plagues befell Egypt. Moses negotiated for the freedom of Israel with plagues of blood, frogs, gnats, flies, locusts, hail, boils, and darkness. However, the plagues did not influence the hardened heart of the Egyptian king. He refused to let God's people go. The last and final plague demands our attention in today's lesson. In order to escape the last plague—the plague of death—there was a plan. The plan included specific details concerning the venue for a meal.

The Plan

Please read Exodus 12:1–30.

 What was the menu and where was it to be prepared? (v. 8)

 What part of this meal preparation would have been most difficult for you?

What is not familiar to us is sometimes extremely hard to understand. Conceptually, dipping herbs into a bowl of blood and painting our doorframes is messy and crude. In fact, the whole drama of a sacrificed lamb may seem bizarre, especially for modern cultures. Nevertheless, consider that day, that era, and that existence. Different emotions emerge, and a different experience.

 What does Exodus 1:7–14 tell us about the people of Israel?

Envision the larger venue—the sights, the smells, the sounds. Clay homes spread over an area broad enough to hold thousands and thousands of families, with sheep and goats in close proximity to the community. The homes had windows with no glass, pots to hold water, and candles or lanterns for light in the night. Farms and gardens provided wheat for bread, and onions and garlic for flavor. Fountains and wells dotted the landscape, and streams etched trails through the sand. The harshness of slavery added a level of pain and fatigue to men and boys, and women and girls.

On the evening of this meal, thousands of lambs were to be slain, roasted, and eaten. Multiple families gathered beneath one roof to comply with what Moses had required—nothing of the lamb should remain until morning. The small homes may have been crowded, but what additional visual stimulus added to the atmosphere and heightened emotion?

Please refer to Exodus 3:21–22, Exodus 11:1–3, and Exodus 12:35–36. As God sent plagues to the Egyptians, he treated the children of Israel with unusual favor. Please describe the effect of his favor.

Can you imagine the conversations amongst the women and girls as they viewed the baskets filled with colorfully embroidered tapestries and woven silks? Imagine how the golden bracelets and goblets oddly sparkled against the backdrop of earthen walls. And the jewels—the children were wearing them.

 As they stood, fully dressed, tending the fire, awaiting the meal, what additional instruction did they all need to follow? (Exodus 12:22–23)

On this night, every Israelite was to remain indoors. This meant that they could not check on their best friends, their neighbors, or their extended family. They needed to keep the children inside—including the boys, including the teenagers. At midnight, when the firstborn sons in all of Egypt died, they could not run out to the cries and screams that they would hear through the windows across the land. They could not leave their homes.

But wait, there is still one more thing included in the atmosphere, packed into each individual venue, and multiplied in the thousands of Jewish homes. It was swelling expectation of hope and belief that God would do what he said he would do.

 What was their anticipation? (Exodus 6:6–7, 7:5)

God had proven himself mighty, able, and present. On what premise did they base their hope? Please read the following verses and briefly note what the children of Israel had experienced.

How were the children of Israel set apart from the Egyptians? How was their experience different?

- ○ Exodus 8:21–24

- ○ Exodus 9:5–7

- ○ Exodus 9:23–26

- ○ Exodus 10:21–23

God knows how to plan a memorable meal. To set the stage and atmosphere, this dinner venue required the mighty hand of God. The plan included the menu and participation. The plan also required a measure of faith. This first Passover meal is probably the most incredible meal ever prepared—and it led to freedom.

Then you will know that I am the LORD your God ...
—Exodus 6:7b (NIV)

THE KITCHEN SINK—REMEMBER THE FLAVOR

Bitter herbs were a required ingredient in the recipe for the Passover meal, and they were common in the Jewish households. Some familiar bitter herbs are chicory, coriander, peppermint, and endive. Other herbs are spicy; some are more fragrant. Specific herbs and spices are identified in most ethnic recipes, and they characterize regional and cultural flavors—flavors that we remember. What herbs and spices are common in your kitchen?

Without looking, list the favorite spices and herbs commonly found in your kitchen.

Note which of these spices or herbs communicate memorable flavors from your childhood or family history. Which memory flavors are missing?

List a dish that you would like to learn to cook. Do you know which seasonings or spices are in the recipe? Please briefly describe how you imagine the food would taste. How would you present this deliciously prepared meal?

Personal Notes:

PART 3: INTRO QUESTION

 What is your preference or idea of a festive dining environment?

Memories of a festive dining experience might include fun and excitement or a particular celebration. Today, we will see that celebrating at meals is a part of God's plan for you. The ambiance, the setting, and the location all play a key role in how we remember these meals.

DESIGN PATTERNS OF CELEBRATION

As we continue to examine the details of the first Passover meal, notice the specific notes of adventure and the visual impressions of the event. These dramatic details later replay as patterns in annual Passover celebrations. They portray God's desire to be known and remembered by his people. God instructs Moses to celebrate with a Passover meal every year; consider the directive in Exodus 12:14.

> And this day shall be unto you for a memorial;
> and ye shall keep it a feast to the LORD
> throughout your generations ...
> —Exodus 12:14 (KJV)

First, let us revisit the Exodus venue. Besides the radiance from the fire, the sizzle of the roasting the lamb, the aroma of unleavened bread, the fragrance of bitter herbs, the sparkle of jewels, and the colorful garments—the celebration plan included props and shoes.

Please read again Exodus 12:1–14.

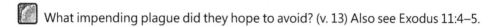 Notice the many details included in these few verses—details designed to remember.

- When was the first Passover meal to take place? (vv. 2, 3, 6)

- To whom was Moses to give these instructions? (v. 3)

- What was the clothing requirement? (v. 11)

- How were they to eat the meal, with what energy? (vv. 10–11)

- What prop was required at the meal? (v. 11)

What impending plague did they hope to avoid? (v. 13) Also see Exodus 11:4–5.

God's chosen people, slaves in Egypt, were preparing for a change of venue. They were to eat the Passover lamb with haste. There would be no time to allow bread dough to rise, so they were to eat unleavened bread. They were to be dressed and ready to go—with shoes on their feet and a staff in their hand. Soon after midnight, there would be a call to action, and the quick departure would require that important items be gathered and ready for travel. However, eating with a staff in hand would be difficult, cumbersome, and awkward. What was so significant about the staff—a simple branch from a tree? Why was the staff a required hand-held prop during the Passover meal? What part would it play, as the story was recited and retold?

Please read Exodus 4:1–5.

In Exodus 3:10, God spoke to Moses from within a burning bush. He said, "So now, go. I am sending you to Pharaoh to bring my people the Israelites out of Egypt." However, Moses was reluctant.

 What does God say in Exodus 4:2?

 What happens to the staff? (Exodus 4:3–4)

Please continue to read Exodus 4:6–17.

 Moses remained unwilling and without confidence. Whom did God send to speak for Moses? (Exodus 4:14–16)

 What did God say about the staff? (Exodus 4:17)

Please read Exodus 7:1–13.

 What was Pharaoh's reaction when Aaron's staff swallowed the other staffs? (Exodus 7:13)

Please read Exodus 8:5–12.

 What part of this staff story would you remember?

Please read Exodus 10:12–20.

 How might this scene grip your emotions?

These are just a few ways that the staff played a role in the Passover story. During the meal, do you think the staff stirred conversation, imagination, and questions from the children? Did the men rehearse the spectacular events of the plagues? Did the women ponder them in their hearts? Did a few rambunctious boys pretend to be Moses, raise their father's staff, and shout, "Let my people go?"

The Israelites gathered treasures, food, and family together for a meal to be remembered. During the meal, they awaited the last plague—the plague that would cause Pharaoh to send them away. They awaited the last plague with staffs in their hands and blood on their doorposts.

Perhaps the most significant detail of the venue was the blood on the doorpost. The blood of a lamb that was slain provided them protection from the final plague. The blood on the doorpost was a signal that death should pass over their home. It was the evidence of faith, their outward expression of hope. It also became an essential part of the story—the story retold every year during the Passover celebration.

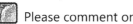 Please read Hebrews 11:23–28. How was faith a part of the Passover story? (Hebrews is near the end of the Bible.)

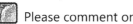 As summarized in Exodus 14:30–31, what was the result of the final plague—the last course of Passover meal?

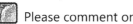 The children had an active role in the Passover tradition. What were the children predicted to do? (Exodus 12:23–27)

The intricate nature of God's plan exceeds anything we can imagine. He planned for his people to celebrate an event that had not yet happened. He layered their story of deliverance with reminders of his mighty hand, and he painted on the doorpost a salvation recipe—a recipe of faith. He provided everything, including the conversation.

Please read Matthew 26:17–20.

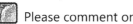 Please comment on how God's celebration plan continued centuries later.

For my thoughts are not your thoughts,
neither are your ways my ways, declares the LORD.
As the heavens are higher than the earth,
so are my ways higher than your ways and
my thoughts than your thoughts.
—Isaiah 55:8–9 (NIV)

THE KITCHEN SINK—OBJECTS OF INTEREST

For today, try an attention-grabbing exercise. Place something unusual in your dining area and see what conversations emerge. Have an objective in mind, even if it is just to see who is paying attention. It does not have to be spiritual in nature or even a teaching point, just a conversation starter. Be prepared with an answer for, "What does this mean?" or "Why is this here?"

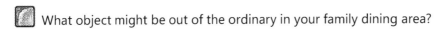 What object might be out of the ordinary in your family dining area?

 What response do you expect?

PART 4: INTRO QUESTION

 Have you ever been very hungry and then had to wait to be served? Briefly describe the circumstances and any insight that you gained from hunger.

WAIT FOR IT

Today's story is about a different type of meal, a meal with the absence of food—a meal that took forty days to serve. The venue·is the wilderness, and the ambiance includes wild animals, angels, and one notorious character. The story exposes the voice of temptation and its design. It also reveals the pattern of transformation and time—the placemat of patience. Do you find it interesting that patience and hunger often go hand in hand?

Please read Matthew 4:1–11

 What was the purpose of this meal event without food? (Matthew 4:1)

 Who planned the venue? (v. 1)

Please read Mark 1:9–13

 Describe the venue and those present during these forty days. (v. 13)

Explore, for a moment, what a desert or wilderness looks like, what it feels like, and what it represents. Imagine being in this desert for forty days, alone, and being very hungry. Please underline phrases from the definition below that stand out to you.

Strong's **Greek Definition for # 2048**

(wilderness, desert) // erhmov // eremos // er'–ay–mos //

AV – wilderness 32, desert 13, desolate 4, solitary 1

solitary, lonely, desolate, uninhabited

a desert, wilderness

deserted places, lonely regions

an uncultivated region fit for pasturage

deserted by others

deprived of the aid and protection of others,

especially of friends, acquaintances, kindred

bereft

To the physical challenges of this location, add the presence of wild animals. What additional emotions might emerge?

With this imagery in mind—the ingredients of a wilderness venue—identify the purpose of each wilderness or desert experience as described in the following verses.

- Numbers 32:13

- Psalm 78:17

- Proverbs 21:19

- Isaiah 40:3

- Revelation 12:6

- Luke 1:80

Did you notice that in every instance, the desert was a prepared place? It was an isolated, uncultivated venue—with purpose. For some, it is a place of rebellion and detention; for others, it is a place of refuge, or a place of nurturing and preparation.

In today's story, we see that after Jesus was baptized, the Spirit immediately led him into the desert. He was there to be tempted—not to rest or to fail, but rather to face the challenge of his eminent foe. Face to face, toe to toe, he wrestled with an evil opponent who sought to divert his faith. Jesus, however, spent time in the wilderness to prove his faith.

Please read again Matthew 4:1–11.

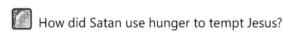 How did Satan use hunger to tempt Jesus?

 How did Jesus respond to the challenge: "If you are the Son of God, turn these stones to bread?" Please write his response. (v. 4)

The phrase "It is written" refers to a verse in Deuteronomy. In the passage, Moses is speaking the Jews who had participated in the first Passover. They had witnessed the plagues in Egypt and crossed the Red Sea on dry land. After they wandered in the wilderness for forty years, Moses spoke the words in Deuteronomy 8:3.

Please read Deuteronomy 8:3.

 Why did God cause the children of Israel to be hungry?

He humbled you, causing you to hunger and then feeding you
with manna, which neither you nor your fathers had known,
to teach you that man does not live on bread alone but on
every word that comes from the mouth of the LORD.
—Deuteronomy 8:3 (NIV)

Please read James 1:2–4.

Why does James call temptation an occasion for joy?

Does joy seem like a strange garnish for temptation? Consider that joy is an ingredient to the recipe for change. What does Romans 12:2 say about transforming and altering our ways?

For a Bit More to Chew On: How might joy require a new or renewed mindset in the midst of trial or a wilderness experience?

How did the desert experience end for Jesus? (Matthew 4:11; Luke 4:13–14)

In this lesson, we explored the wilderness venue—not as a woeful place, but rather as an inevitable, purposeful venue that we will travel through and dine in. The menu will vary. The food may be supernatural, like manna, or delivered by angels; it may be prepared in your kitchen or in the house of a stranger. Nevertheless, it is a place where the spiritual food of God's Word is the nourishment we need. Food in the desert venue is always best eaten with patience and joy.

One last bite: During our brief wilderness study, did you consider the wild animals—the external scary creatures that emerge stealthily and unexpectedly when food is around? Did you consider that there were angels there as well?

Personal Observation:

> Beloved, think it not strange concerning the fiery trial which is to try you, as though some strange thing happened unto you: But rejoice, inasmuch as ye are partakers of Christ's sufferings; that, when his glory shall be revealed, ye may be glad also with exceeding joy.
> —1 Peter 4:12–13 (KJV)

THE KITCHEN SINK—PREPARE FOR ACTION

Prepare your mind for action, and create a pattern of rejoicing. A pattern starts with an idea or goal, which, when implemented, is repeated, and then repeated again. Try this pattern activity; set your table with purpose.

Set your table as an expression of hope. Set it well before it is time to eat, in anticipation of what good things are to come. Let it remind you of your purpose and the desire of your heart. Consider what your table setting says to those who will be joining you for the meal. Sometimes joy takes a little motivation, so remember to smile.

How did this intentional expression of hope influence you?

PART 5: INTRO QUESTION

Have you ever carefully planned a meal celebration, considered every detail, and still encountered a huge miscalculation? Briefly note.

BEHOLD THE BEST

As we have seen, the venue is an integral part of every meal. An upper room—prepared for an intimate, private, and memorable occasion—staged the Last Supper. The Passover meal, eaten in the homes of Egyptian slaves, repelled a terrible plague. Angels, in a solitary wilderness setting, served Jesus when he was tempted. The venue was significant for each of these meals and important to the story and its relevance.

In this lesson, as we take a glimpse into a particular wedding in Galilee, think about the location—a banquet setting—and the preparations that preceded the brief window of time. While we do not know the bride or the groom, we will see how a few guests had a delicious impact on their celebration.

Please read John 2:1–11 to discover how the banquet hall was the perfect stage for a grand event.

Who was at the wedding? Please list all those mentioned.

What was the miscalculation in planning?

What did Mary say to the servants? (v. 5)

At the time of the wedding, Jesus had yet to perform miracles publicly. Even while hungry and being tempted in the wilderness, he refused to turn stones into bread. However, people were choosing to follow him; they were curious about him, and they drew near to hear his teachings.

When Jesus instructs the servants, how do they respond?

What did the servants know about the 120–180 gallons of wine? Who was excluded from this information?

What was the result of this miracle? (John 2:11b)

How often do we see something and later question ourselves, wondering if it was real? Did our minds play a trick on us? Did *that* actually happen? What was it about this event that sealed the deal for his disciples; what caused them to believe?

To broaden our perspective, let us look into the backstory of those who witnessed this miracle. One story revolves around John the Baptist, as told by the Apostle John.

To clarify, John the Baptist and Apostle John are not the same person. Jesus and John the Baptist were cousins—they were only a few months apart in age, and their mothers knew each other well. On the other hand, Apostle John was one of the twelve disciples. He was a friend of Jesus, and he wrote five of the books in the Bible. It is believed that Apostle John, while not mentioned in the passage, told this wedding story from a firsthand perspective—that is, he attended the wedding, and he witnessed these events.

Please read John 1:28–2:2.

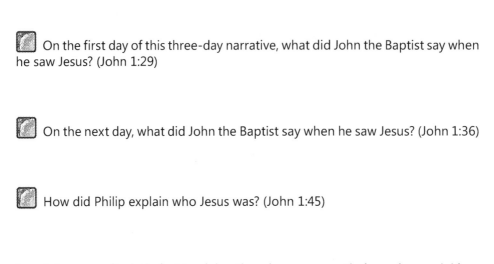

On the first day of this three-day narrative, what did John the Baptist say when he saw Jesus? (John 1:29)

On the next day, what did John the Baptist say when he saw Jesus? (John 1:36)

How did Philip explain who Jesus was? (John 1:45)

Israel long awaited their Messiah—the chosen one, their savior and king. Nathanael knew what Philip meant, at least partially. The Lamb of God correlates to the Passover lamb. Recall, from Exodus 12, the lamb eaten during the Passover meal. A lamb without blemish was slain, and its blood was painted on the doorpost of each Jewish home. Death passed over those homes, and the people escaped the final plague of death. John the Baptist was announcing that Jesus is the Passover lamb.

His announcement was:

> Look, the Lamb of God, who takes away the sin of the world!
> —John 1:29 (NIV)

As you respond to the following questions, try to relate to the daily activities of these men, with the backdrop of ancient Galilee and this world-changing announcement.

Two men, who followed John the Baptist, understood this introduction. Who were they, and what did they do? (John 1:37–42)

What did Jesus say to the two men in John 1:43–51?

 What happened on the third day? (John 2:1–2)

Please list the four disciples who attended the wedding with Jesus. Also, include John, since he wrote this account.

To understand additional relationship dynamics present at the wedding, please read Luke 2:40–52. These verses take us back about eighteen years—the child is Jesus.

What was Mary's reaction to the developing character and role of her son? (Luke 2:51)

Mary knew that Jesus was someone special. After John's decree—"Behold the Lamb of God"—Mary knew her son's destiny was unfolding before her eyes. The disciples were convinced that Jesus was someone exceptional. They followed him, and they witnessed his appeal. Can you imagine the energy amongst the disciples, an energy filled with rare and unspeakable anticipation and wonder? However, Jesus was different on this day. Something had happened that moved him into the full anointing, into the power of his ministry, into the willingness and freedom to go public.

Please read Luke 3:21–23 and read again John 1:32–34.

What do these verses tell us?

Please recall, from the last lesson, the story of Jesus in the wilderness. After being tempted, what was evident in his life? (Luke 4:13–14)

John baptized Jesus in the Jordan. Then Jesus fasted and prayed for forty days and nights. When he returned to Galilee, in the power of the Spirit, he attended a wedding. Mary, a few disciples, six large stone water pots, many gallons of the best wine, servants, and power were present. In a venue where there was something lacking, the disciples put their faith in Jesus. The miracle included God's presence as people gathered for a meal to celebrate.

Here I am! I stand at the door and knock. If anyone hears my voice
and opens the door, I will come in and eat with him, and he with me.
—Revelation 3:20 (NIV)

THE KITCHEN SINK—FAVORITE FLAVOR

The governor of the feast called the bridegroom and said, "This wine is better." What makes wine better? What makes food better? Is it the flavor, the aroma, the colors, or the texture? Or does the venue and circumstance make it better? Of course, it is all things combined. The taste-and-see approach leads us to our favorites.

 As you prepare for the **Group Taste-and-See Experience**, please review the following list of spice mixtures. Some have ancient roots, some are exotic, and some have a modern twist to accommodate the marketplace. Choose several, and research to discover which spices and herbs combine to produce that specific flavor.

- Creole (American Colonies)
- Baharat (Middle East)
- Berbere (Ethiopia and Eritrea)
- Chaat masala (India and Pakistan)
- Chipotle (Mexico)
- Curry (India)
- Cajun (New Orleans, USA)
- Five-spice (China)
- Garam Masala (South Asia)
- Herbes de Provence (France)
- Harissa (North Africa)
- Hawaij (Yemen)
- Khmeli-Suneli (Georgia, USSR)
- Jerk spice (Jamaica)
- Masala (South Asia)
- Mixed spice (United Kingdom)
- Old Bay seasoning (USA)
- Panch phoron (India and Bangladesh)
- Pumpkin pie spice (USA)
- Quatre épices (France)
- Ranch seasoning (USA)
- Ras el hanout (North Africa)
- Shichimi togarashi (Japan)
- Taco spice (USA)

Please note your findings. Feel free to add a spice mixture not listed.

Please review the next page to prepare for the Group Taste-and-See Experience.

Group Taste-and-See Experience

SHARE A FLAVOR: SAUCES AND DIPS

In many cultures, dips are traditional and shared with others at the table. An intimate interaction takes place when people eat from the same bowl or plate. Offering a bite from your personal plate relates an even deeper level of relationship. Sometimes etiquette prohibits this, but we can all relate to the shared experience.

For the **Group Taste-and-See Experience,** use a spice mixture to make a dip or sauce to share with the group. If you use a packaged mix, take the package to the group gathering for display and discussion. If you prepare a mix from a recipe, take samples of the herb and spice ingredients to the group session. Be prepared to arrange your ingredients on a sample dish. As a group, you will discuss the flavors and colors of the individual components and the combinations. Be sure to include something to dip, such as bread, cooked sausages, or vegetables.

DISCUSSION SUGGESTIONS

- Sample the spices that are unfamiliar to you. Consider how many herbs and spices are bitter or unpleasant if served alone, but the infusion of their flavor adds a depth and richness to the finished dish.
- Compare packaged products to ready-made bottled dips or sauces. Compare dried herb and spice mixes to fresh versions of the same ingredients.
- Discuss the cost of the various spice mixtures—with relationship to quality— for the premixed packages, fresh, and dried ingredients.
- Compare overall appearance and enjoyment of each version.
- Discuss new insights to spice as it relates to memory.

Celebrate with Flavors to Remember

The invitation is an integral part of every meal—the call to eat. The best meal invitations have an essence like that of bread; the aroma, substance, and texture of words invite us to taste and enjoy, compelling us to dine. In this chapter, we will study invitations and their relationship to the meal. We will explore how the motive, the backstory, and the ripple effect flavor each response.

And Jesus said unto them, I am the bread of life ...
—John 6:35 (KJV)

THE INVITATION

- Objective: Demonstrate that an invitation is a personal request for your presence.
- Bible Topic: Attendance is the responsibility of the guest.
- Meal Topic: The voice, aroma, and visual cues all compliment the call to dinner.
- Food Topic: Yeast
- Food to be Prepared: Bread

PART 1: INTRO QUESTION

When you receive an invitation, what makes it compelling, what causes anticipation, and what motivates you to have a positive response?

The simplest and perhaps most profound invitation is expressed in one word: *come*. "Please come" adds a personal appeal and touch of etiquette. A dinner invitation can be formal and presented in a silver-lined envelope, or it can be a text message to the family room; it can be an e-vite or an e-mail, a phone call or a holler from the kitchen. Not all invitations are to dinner, but they all should include certain information. "Come and eat" suggests more than simply attending—it implies a measure of participation. An invitation should include time and location, spoken or implied; it should also grab your attention and generate interest. Invitations have a voice—the tone, enthusiasm or lack thereof, and timing are ultimately crucial to the response. The response to an invitation, however, is always the responsibility of the recipient, the one to whom the invitation is extended.

WHAT IS SPLENDOR WITHOUT YOU?

In this lesson, we will consider four banquet invitations from the book of Esther. The main characters in these first banquet stories are King Xerxes, Queen Vashti, seven chamberlains, and seven princes. Some of the names might be a little hard to read or pronounce. Try to relate to them as people whom are recognized by the king, and whose names made it into a small little book before Job, Psalms, and Proverbs. Please note: King Xerxes also translates to read *King Ahasuerus*, depending on the Bible translation.

Please read Esther 1:1–20.

From 486–465 BC, King Xerxes ruled the Persian Empire. In the third year of his reign, whom did he invite to the first banquet? (v. 3)

What was the king's motive for the first feast? (v. 4)

Whom did King Xerxes initially invite to a second banquet, which occurred six months later? (v. 5)

What stands out to you about the venue and atmosphere of the second banquet? Please use words that paint a visual picture of this seven-day event. (vv. 5–8)

To whom did Queen Vashti extend the third banquet invitation? (v. 9)

From your own entertaining experience or observations, describe the role Queen Vashti *may have* played during her banquet.

What was the king's final attendance request? (vv. 10–11)

There are several ways to look at these invitations and the intentions of the king and queen. King Xerxes was evidently very successful, and his celebrations were well attended. He had a beautiful queen and great wealth. During these festivals, everyone—from the greatest to the least—saw and experienced the power and glory of his reign. So why did Vashti refuse to attend?

Of course, we can only speculate what Queen Vashti was thinking, but please list several possibilities.

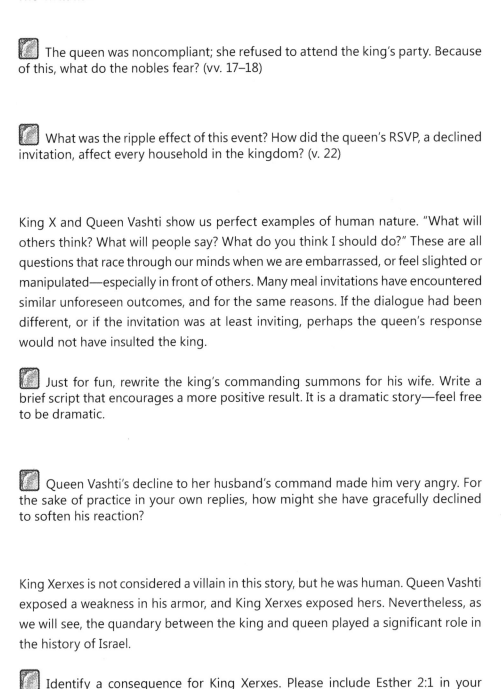

The queen was noncompliant; she refused to attend the king's party. Because of this, what do the nobles fear? (vv. 17–18)

What was the ripple effect of this event? How did the queen's RSVP, a declined invitation, affect every household in the kingdom? (v. 22)

King X and Queen Vashti show us perfect examples of human nature. "What will others think? What will people say? What do you think I should do?" These are all questions that race through our minds when we are embarrassed, or feel slighted or manipulated—especially in front of others. Many meal invitations have encountered similar unforeseen outcomes, and for the same reasons. If the dialogue had been different, or if the invitation was at least inviting, perhaps the queen's response would not have insulted the king.

Just for fun, rewrite the king's commanding summons for his wife. Write a brief script that encourages a more positive result. It is a dramatic story—feel free to be dramatic.

Queen Vashti's decline to her husband's command made him very angry. For the sake of practice in your own replies, how might she have gracefully declined to soften his reaction?

King Xerxes is not considered a villain in this story, but he was human. Queen Vashti exposed a weakness in his armor, and King Xerxes exposed hers. Nevertheless, as we will see, the quandary between the king and queen played a significant role in the history of Israel.

Identify a consequence for King Xerxes. Please include Esther 2:1 in your response.

Please read Philippians 2:3–4.

When the king's anger subsided, he remembered Vashti. He remembered her beauty. He remembered she was gone. Consider how the perspective found in Philippians 2:3–4 might have changed the outcome for this royal marriage. Please note personal insight.

The words in an invitation are like ingredients in a recipe. If one ingredient is omitted or mismeasured, or if our recipe is wrong, repeating the error will not improve the results. As we continue, in the Book of Esther, we will see a different invitation approach. We will see how planning and prayer can ultimately affect the outcome of every meal invitation.

> Do nothing out of selfish ambition or vain conceit,
> but in humility consider others better than yourselves.
> Each of you should look not only to your own interests,
> but also to the interests of others.
> —Philippians 2:3–4 (NIV)

THE KITCHEN SINK—OKAY, MAYBE

Please evaluate a dining invitation (casual or formal) that you refused or declined. Briefly note reasons you chose not to attend.

What slight alteration might have changed your response? Please note: There is no obligation to share personal answers.

Part 2: Intro Question

 Have you ever extended an invitation with uncertainty? Briefly explain, and note the tone of your voice or the emotion in your heart.

Today, we will be reading about a beautiful young Jewish girl named Esther. Please recall, from the last lesson, the story of Queen Vashti and her refusal to obey the king's command. Once Vashti was banished from his sight, King Xerxes sought a new beauty to replace her. After potential brides spent twelve months in pampered preparations, the king chose Esther to wear the royal crown. As the queen, she also held banquets in their Persian palace. For our study, we will focus on the invitations.

Haman and Mordecai are two additional key characters in this saga. Haman, the king's highest noble, hated Mordecai. Esther grew up under Mordecai's care; she was like a daughter to him. Also, please remember that King Xerxes is sometimes translated *King Ahasuerus*, depending on the Bible you read.

In a similar way that Jews in Egypt lived segregated during their slavery to Pharaoh, Jews in the Persian culture were also set apart, although it appears that they did live amongst each other in the provinces. King Xerxes was not a Jew, and Mordecai commanded Esther to keep her Jewish heritage a secret. It was this secret and an evil plot that led to the first invitation in today's lesson.

Please Come

Please read Esther 3:1–15 to discover Haman's wicked scheme.

What convincing opinion did Haman voice to King Xerxes? (v. 8)

Esther 3:1–5 briefly details Haman's backstory and motive for destroying the Jews. Please identify the emotion evident in his motive. (v. 5)

Please continue to read Esther 4:1–5:8. As you read, embrace the text as you would a novel. Engage your thoughts to experience the sounds and surroundings. Hear the voices of the characters and the inflections of their words. Note the texture of their clothing, and sense the emotion of their hearts.

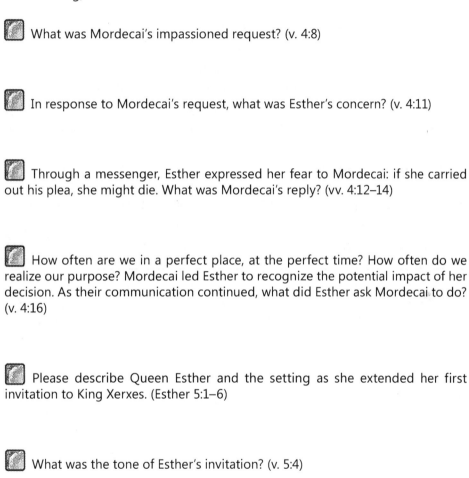 What was Mordecai's impassioned request? (v. 4:8)

In response to Mordecai's request, what was Esther's concern? (v. 4:11)

Through a messenger, Esther expressed her fear to Mordecai: if she carried out his plea, she might die. What was Mordecai's reply? (vv. 4:12–14)

How often are we in a perfect place, at the perfect time? How often do we realize our purpose? Mordecai led Esther to recognize the potential impact of her decision. As their communication continued, what did Esther ask Mordecai to do? (v. 4:16)

Please describe Queen Esther and the setting as she extended her first invitation to King Xerxes. (Esther 5:1–6)

What was the tone of Esther's invitation? (v. 5:4)

How did King Xerxes respond to her invitation? (vv. 5:5–6)

Even though King Xerxes seemed very generous and even eager to please, Esther remained humble, and she extended a second invitation.

The Invitation

📷 Please describe the setting of the second invitation. Who was there? What were they doing? (v. 5:8)

A lot can happen in three days. Our worlds can turn upside down, or incredible victories can be won. Before Esther approached the king, she asked Mordecai to bring together all the Jews in Susa (Shushan) to fast for her. They fasted for three days and nights. She also fasted with her maids. After three days without a meal, Esther put on her royal robes. She waited for the king to acknowledge her presence; she then extended an invitation to dine. The invitation itself would set the stage for deliverance, yet Esther was not presumptuous with a plea for her life. Instead, she invited him again to yet another banquet. "If it pleases the king," she said.

Was Esther building up courage, or was she reading between the lines that the timing was not right? Did she understand how patience works or how mystery might allure the king's attention? Maybe there was a still-small voice prompting her to wait. Perhaps not everything was ready.

📷 Please continue to read Esther 5:8–14. Consider Haman's attitude and his response to the dual invitations. The king offered Esther up to half the kingdom. How did Haman respond?

With gallows built for Mordecai, and a decree to annihilate every Jew at stake, Esther prepared a second banquet for her enemy and the king. For a third time, King Xerxes asked, "What is your request?" This time Esther answered, and her response had a powerful impact on the meal, on the mood, and on the dinner guests.

📷 Since a meal is not complete until the conversation is over, please read Esther 7:1–10, and record what happened at the banquet for each individual.

○ Queen Esther

○ King Xerxes /Ahasuerus

○ Haman

Why do you think Esther extended an invitation to Haman?

Esther exposed Haman's evil plot, and she continued to find favor in the presence of the king. We do not want to spoil the end of the story, but things worked out for the Jews. You should know that after the battle and Jewish victory, a decree made feasting, celebrating with joy, and giving gifts an annual Jewish holiday. Haman, of course, was unable to attend.

The king's heart *is* in the hand of the LORD ...
—Proverbs 21:1 (KJV)

THE KITCHEN SINK—SET THE STAGE

The goal of Esther's invitation was to deliver her people from impending disaster. She also hoped to save her own life. Realize that the original cause for alarm remained, but after Esther entered the courtyard—with an invitation to dine—the king provided a way of escape. Esther's invitation started with prayer, and it included the preparation of her heart. Her invitation also had a visual component: dressed in her royal robes, Esther stood in view of the king.

What identifies your invitation patterns? Is it comfortable chairs or flowers on the table? Is it the steamed-up windows from simmering pots on a crisp fall day? Is it the way food is prepared, or is it a friendly face?

 Note what you discover to be inviting as you walk around your home, a restaurant, or another meal venue.

 What is your goal as you invite family or friends to the table?

And who knows but that you have come to royal position
for such a time as this?
—Esther 4:14b (NIV)

PART 3: INTRO QUESTION

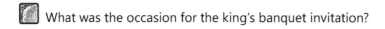 Have you ever declined an invitation because you did not have a suitable outfit or because you simply did not want to wear the required clothes? Please briefly explain.

Invitations will quite often indicate appropriated dress, if not directly then indirectly. Appropriate might be black tie, flip-flops, or any style in between. Whichever the case, the fashion obligation is usually suggested or implied. Today we are going to look at a parable and several invitations to a feast—a feast hosted by another king. As you read the story, consider what you might wear to such an event, and why. Consider the backstories of all involved, including the backstory of the king.

COME DRESSED FOR DINNER

Please read Matthew 22:1–14

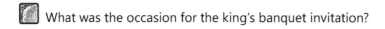 What was the occasion for the king's banquet invitation?

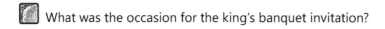 Describe the king's three invitations in verses 3–10.

- ○ Verse 3

- ○ Verse 4

- ○ Verse 10

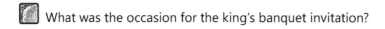 Who delivered the invitations?

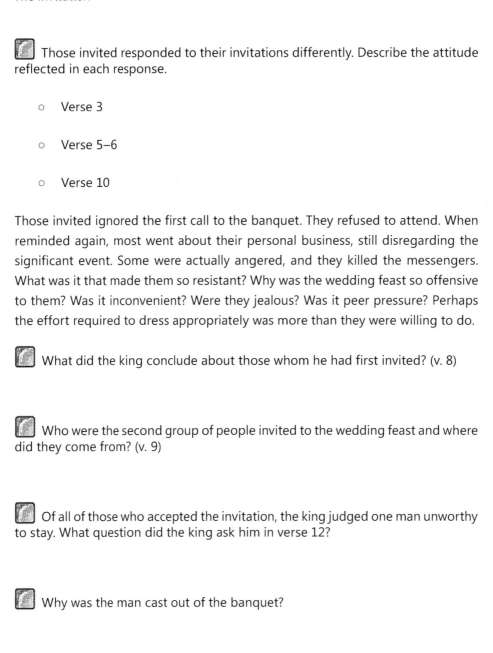 Those invited responded to their invitations differently. Describe the attitude reflected in each response.

- o   Verse 3

- o   Verse 5–6

- o   Verse 10

Those invited ignored the first call to the banquet. They refused to attend. When reminded again, most went about their personal business, still disregarding the significant event. Some were actually angered, and they killed the messengers. What was it that made them so resistant? Why was the wedding feast so offensive to them? Was it inconvenient? Were they jealous? Was it peer pressure? Perhaps the effort required to dress appropriately was more than they were willing to do.

What did the king conclude about those whom he had first invited? (v. 8)

Who were the second group of people invited to the wedding feast and where did they come from? (v. 9)

Of all of those who accepted the invitation, the king judged one man unworthy to stay. What question did the king ask him in verse 12?

Why was the man cast out of the banquet?

A parable is like a parallel story. It helps us relate to the unfamiliar with a story that we can easily understand. In order to relate to this story, identify what kingdom era you thought about when you read this parable. Also, consider the clothing of that era. Did you think of a renaissance wedding, with hooped gowns and feathered hats? Did you think of a feast in ancient Rome, with togas and sandals? Perhaps your kingdom reference is fairy-tale-like, with Prince Charming searching for his bride. Perhaps it was a vague impression of a lonely king in a dry and sandy land.

 Describe your image of the king's kingdom in this parable. What venue did you think about when you read this story? (There is no right or wrong answer.)

Consider for a moment the palace in Queen Esther's story. Please read again Esther 1:1–8.

 The palace in Esther's story was impressive. It was prepared in magnificent splendor for banquets, and it was prepared for all of the people. How does the image of Esther's palace enlarge your idea of the king's personal investment—the king in Matthew 22:1–14?

We understand invitations to wedding banquets. We also understand how to respond properly to an invitation. We have all ignored an invitation from time to time, and we have refused to attend for untold reasons. Nevertheless, why would someone ignore an invitation to eat with the king?

 Please note a few excuses that come to mind.

It is not hard to come up with a reason or a whole variety of excuses, especially if the request requires some yielding on our part. According to the parable, there was a clothing expectation. Clothing is personal; it is a visual expression of who we are. Once again, consider the kingdom era that you related to in the previous questions. For that era, imagine the clothing worn by the people mentioned in Matthew 22:9–10. Just imagine, if you were one of the people on the street, would you be prepared to dress for the wedding?

For a Bit More to Chew On: Please read the following verses and comment on how one might respond to an invitation with these wardrobe requirements.

- Zachariah 3:3–5 (second to last book in the Old Testament)

- Isaiah 61:10 (around the middle of the Bible)

- Revelation 19:7–8 (the last book of the Bible)

- Revelation 7:14

It may seem like the wardrobe in these verses is elusive or unattainable. However, with God, all things are possible. It may appear that the parable in Matthew 22 is about an angry king, a series of refused invitations, and a strict dress code. However, a closer look reveals a wedding hall filled with guests. The guests are dressed and dine at a fabulous celebration prepared by the king. Their garments reflect the king's regard for the intimate details of every guest, as a provision for his son. The king had a plan. He continued to extend an invitation until he completely filled his banquet hall.

Briefly note your thoughts:

THE KITCHEN SINK—SOUNDS SO GOOD

Today's parable started with the words "The kingdom of heaven is like ..." Another parable—which remarkably includes a recipe—starts with the same words: "The kingdom of heaven is like yeast" (Matthew 13:33 NIV).

Yeast is what makes bread smell so good. The yeast expands and causes the dough to rise. While baking, little air pockets in the dough release the sweet, fresh-baked scent. Experienced bakers use the properties of yeast to make delicious bread. Their process may appear effortless, yet they instinctively feel the texture and the temperature of the dough. They know how and when to adjust their recipe. Their skill takes time to develop, and yet the aroma from fresh-baked bread, whether produced by a chef or countertop bread maker, is what invites us to experience its flavor.

In a similar way, the aroma of an invitation enhances the call to dinner. Like a baker who modifies a recipe, we can modify the delivery of an invitation and adapt to the ingredients of life.

To get a clearer focus of your invitation style, identify the series of events that generally occur around your dinnertime. Please briefly include relevant family or friend involvement, food preparation, electronic devices, schedules, and the energy level of your household.

The king's goal was to celebrate the marriage of his son with a full banquet hall. What is your goal for dinner?

Realizing that we cannot control everything or anyone—except maybe ourselves—what modification might improve your invitation delivery? Comment on the way you give or respond to the call to dinner.

The kingdom of heaven is like yeast that a woman took and mixed into a large amount of flour until it worked all through the dough.
—Matthew 13:33 (NIV)

PART 4: INTRO QUESTION

🔲 Have you ever declined an invitation because of someone else or peer pressure? Briefly explain.

It may not be possible to attend every event or to accept every invitation. Most likely, wisdom has prevented us from attending some events. Nevertheless, some invitations we decline because of opposition from family or friends, or because of the expense. What happens when the party is over and we realize the sacrifice or effort would have been worth it? Did we surrender too easily to the opposition? Regrettably, we want a do-over. Really, can we just wind back the clock? Please.

RSVP

The parables in this lesson include choices, reasons, and excuses. As you read about these people, consider their backstories. Consider who influenced their decisions or who demanded their attention.

Imagine your own response to these invitations. Ultimately, your response would determine if you would be inside or outside—at the party or not. Consider the differing venues; consider those who entered the banquet and those who remained outside. What would it look like from each vantage point—inside or out? How might your choice make you feel? Imagine how the food would taste.

Please read Luke 14:15–24. Jesus sat with lawyers and Pharisees as he told this tale.

🔲 List three excuses made when the servants announced that the banquet was ready.

1.

2.

3.

What does Luke 14:24 suggest about the consequence of their excuses?

The man who prepared this great banquet must have had complete confidence in his chef. The consequence was not missing the party, not missing the social event of the day, or not seeing the who's who among the kingdom set. The consequence was that they would not taste his banquet. What does that mean? What remarkable flavors did they not get to enjoy? We can use our imagination—but the answer is a mystery.

 Please read Matthew 13:34–35. Complete the following verses (NIV).

(v. 34) Jesus spoke all these things to the crowd in parables;

_____

_____

(v.35b) "I will utter things hidden _____."

The relationship parallels between the kingdom of heaven and banquets on earth contain a mystery. As we study the missed meal opportunities, there are clues that give us some understanding. The additional image of wardrobe and the taste of delicious food broadens our perspective beyond a simple tale to a personal reality. However, the compelling point is our response; the invitation to dine requires a response. Every invitation we extend or receive is like a dress rehearsal to the heavenly coming attraction. Consider the question asked in Matthew 24:3. Jesus responds with another banquet parable in the next chapter.

 What did the disciples ask in Matthew 24:3?

The Invitation

Please read Matthew 25:1–13. This parable is in response to the question, "What will be the sign of your coming and of the end of the age?" (Matthew 24:3 NIV)

Please list the characters mentioned in Matthew 25:1–13.

How was the invitation announcement delivered? (Matthew 25:6)

Please describe everything you can about the setting when the bridegroom arrives: the time of day, the building, etc.

All ten virgins received invitations to the banquet. What set them apart from each other? What made five of them wise? Please note that the foolish virgins did not ask to borrow money.

Most likely, none of these young women were the bride, but as a part of the wedding procession, they planned to greet the groom. They were to usher him in, according to *Matthew Henry Commentary on the Whole Bible* (1721).

It would have been common to carry a lamp with oil and to carry enough oil to light the way throughout the night. Midnight was the end of the day, but only halfway into the night. The five foolish virgins were not even minimally prepared to meet the bridegroom. They carried lamps with no oil. Apparently, the groom expected more. Their garments required an accessory: a lamp with oil to light the way.

The five wise virgins entered into the wedding banquet with the guest of honor. As it relates to the kingdom of heaven, they are about to experience something incredible.

Please read 1 Corinthians 2:6–10.

Please complete the phrase: 1 Corinthians 2:9 (NIV)

No eye _____

no ear _____

no mind _____

what God has prepared _____.

Note new insights into the kingdom of heaven and its celestial feast.

"Blessed are those who are invited to
the wedding supper of the Lamb!
... These are the true words of God."
—Revelation 19:9 (NIV)

THE KITCHEN SINK—DEFINE BY DESIGN

Choose one thing that you can do that will make the entry into your home more inviting. This can be as simple as sweeping the front porch or tying a ribbon on the doorknob. If you are ready for a challenge, spend some time looking at your front door or entry to your home. Observe what others see. From what they see, what might they anticipate, and what assumptions might they make? What is it about your entry that invites your family and friends to come and see?

Note your observations and intentions.

PART 5: INTRO QUESTION

Save-the-dates are a pre-notification of an upcoming event, sent or extended prior to the formal invitation. Why do you think save-the-date announcements have become so popular?

Save-the-dates set in motion the countdown for being ready to go. That countdown can generate anticipation or apprehension. Save-the-dates inform you that something of importance calls for your attention, and the host is making every effort to insure your presence. You might ask yourself, "What do I need to do to get ready?"

The last two meal invitations in the Bible include save-the-dates. These save-the-dates are for two quite different tables, yet the same host extends them. For many, these announcements remain unopened, unread, and unrealized. The first date is for another wedding banquet—the second is not. The first requires proper wedding attire—the second implies, "Come as you are." The first banquet call patiently lingers in time—the second has an appointed time. The invitation to the first banquet requires an RSVP, with names written in the book. The second requires no reply; however, the accommodations have been prearranged.

Many know at least something about the first of these events, the wedding supper of the Lamb. The second meal is a little more obscure, less talked about: the great supper of God. In casual consideration, these two meals might be confused as the same event or at least complementary events, like the rehearsal dinner before the wedding and main reception. The great supper of God sounds like a big bowl of hot stew served with warm buttery bread, but it is not. The first event is going to be grand—the second banquet has a terrible menu. Revelation 19 reveals both invitations. For now, we will only study the first.

SAVE THE DATE

Revelation is a book of prophecy. Written after the resurrection of Jesus, the book of Revelation foretells what is to come, detailing future events in heaven and on earth. It contains warnings and blessings. It is also very graphic in nature, with many things hard to understand. Ultimately, it is a glimpse into amazing. Take your time to appreciate the heavenly details. Remember, God gave them to us for a reason and purpose. Please read Revelation 1:1–3 to find the benefit of reading the story in today's lesson.

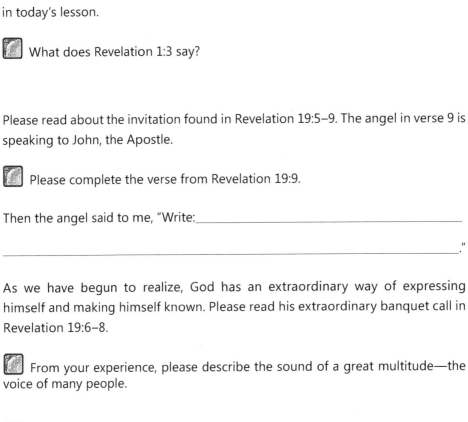 What does Revelation 1:3 say?

Please read about the invitation found in Revelation 19:5–9. The angel in verse 9 is speaking to John, the Apostle.

Please complete the verse from Revelation 19:9.

Then the angel said to me, "Write:_____

_____."

As we have begun to realize, God has an extraordinary way of expressing himself and making himself known. Please read his extraordinary banquet call in Revelation 19:6–8.

From your experience, please describe the sound of a great multitude—the voice of many people.

From you memory, recall the roar of rushing waters. What energy does that sound express to you?

Loud thunder follows the brilliant flashes of lightning in the sky. The concussion of the sound affects more than our ears; it is felt as it approaches and travels through the atmosphere. Please briefly describe the sensation that the peals of loud thunder bring to you.

A great multitude implies a large expanse, space enough to contain a crowd with merging sounds and activities. Rushing waters are on the ground beneath, traveling over the crevices and terrain of the earth. Thunder is in the sky above, with its distance marked in time. All have volume, and power, and a vast presence. It is with this heavenly megaphone that the words in these verses are proclaimed.

 What is the announcement in Revelation 19:7?

Imagine the voice of the multitude, the power of rushing water, and the crescendo of thunder as this first hallelujah is spoken, as the call is initiated, and the announcement made.

> "Hallelujah! ... the wedding of the Lamb has come,
> and his bride has made herself ready. . ."
> —Revelation 19:6–7 (NIV)

After such an announcement, would you choose to attend? Would you save the date? Would you slip on your wedding shoes and with eager expectation await the celebration?

Perhaps you need a little more information. The Lamb is the groom, the Lamb of God. Recall from earlier lessons, Jesus is the Lamb of God.

 Please take a moment to list what you know about Jesus.

Now, let us take a closer look at the bride; the wedding has come, and she has made herself ready.

 What was given to the bride to wear? Revelation 19:8

Wait, there is a little more. Please read Revelation 21:9–27.

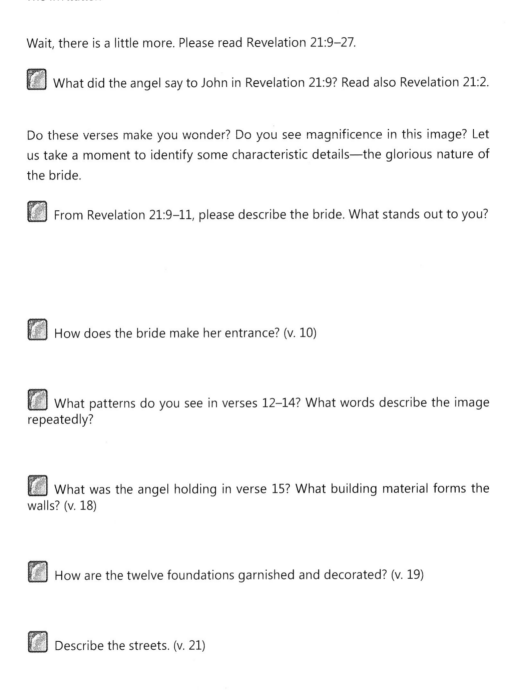 What did the angel say to John in Revelation 21:9? Read also Revelation 21:2.

Do these verses make you wonder? Do you see magnificence in this image? Let us take a moment to identify some characteristic details—the glorious nature of the bride.

From Revelation 21:9–11, please describe the bride. What stands out to you?

How does the bride make her entrance? (v. 10)

What patterns do you see in verses 12–14? What words describe the image repeatedly?

What was the angel holding in verse 15? What building material forms the walls? (v. 18)

How are the twelve foundations garnished and decorated? (v. 19)

Describe the streets. (v. 21)

Who is in the city and who is not? (vv. 22–27)

What stands out to you in this description of the bride, the wife of the Lamb? Is it the mystery of the city? Is it the thousands of miles of sparkling jewels that decorate the skirts of her foundation, or is it the golden rod that measures this brilliant dwelling place?

She descends from heaven, fully adorned for her husband. Imagine *this* wedding banquet venue filled with guests.

Personal Notes:

The Spirit and the bride say, "Come!"
—Revelation 22:17a (NIV)

THE KITCHEN SINK—A LOVE NOTE

The marriage of the Lamb and his bride is a love story. The marriage supper is a celebration in spectacular fashion. In our most vivid imaginations, we cannot possibly grasp the depth and splendor of this event, and yet we are a part of the story. We are included in the narrative, the setting, and the preparations. Love sets the stage for our involvement.

With this in mind, plan a meal that reads like a note expressing love to your family or friends. Please use your imagination for a memorable occasion. This may not be a meal you ever present; however, it may inspire you in your day-to-day.

Describe the setting.

How would you invite your guests to the table?

What would you serve?

What would you hope they remember?

Personal Notes:

Please review the next page to prepare for the Group Taste-and-See Experience.

Group Taste-and-See Experience

SENSE THE WELCOME: BREAD

As we briefly discussed, the aroma of bread is like an invitation to dine. For the group event, prepare or purchase fresh-baked bread. There are many options for this. You may choose a recipe that requires hand kneading or a recipe designed for a bread maker. Frozen, ready-to-bake dough can rise quickly in a warm oven and then be baked and served warm during class. Choose what best suits your experience, time, and budget. If you have never made home-baked bread, take this opportunity to expand your experience. Perfection is not the goal; experience is.

As a class, it would be most enjoyable for you to serve bread warm from the oven. Include butter, honey, another spread, cheese, or meat to compliment the experience.

DISCUSSION SUGGESTIONS

- As you taste each presentation, discuss the subtle characteristics—the aroma, the textures, and the satisfaction.
- Discuss the pros and cons of fresh-baked and commercial breads.
- Discuss the cultural and marketing biases that prevent us from embracing the gift of bread.
- Include in your discussion John 6:48, where Jesus said, "I am the bread of life." What does that verse mean to you?
- What do you find inviting about Jesus?

The table and chairs are an intimate detail of every meal venue. Our place at the table is personal—a space reserved for us by custom, or tradition, or a predetermined relationship pattern. Not every table is a peaceful place; not every table shares laughter. However, every table includes the spiritual implication of good versus evil; with that always comes a bit of drama. The standard of bliss is an artificial one, as the day of no tears has not yet come. In the meantime, the stage is set for courage, hope, and some great fun. Enjoy the perspective of this chapter. It is probably different from what you expect.

> So Mephibosheth ate at David's table
> like one of the king's sons.
> —2 Samuel 9:11 (NIV)

THE TABLE AND CHAIRS

- Objective: Embrace the personalities and relationship patterns at our table.
- Bible Topic: He prepares a table for me, in the presence of my enemies.
- Meal Topic: Setting the table/dishes
- Bible Food: Oil and vinegar
- Food to be Prepared: Appetizers

PART 1: INTRO QUESTION

 Where is your favorite place to sit at the dinner table? Briefly explain why.

Have you ever noticed how dinner scenes in a movie enrich the plot and move the story forward? Consider how meal scenes are usually the backdrop for revealing new and often important information.

For instance, a scene that opens with a close-up of trembling fingers grasping a chipped and stained teacup might suggest someone is cold, scared, or feeble. The cup might be a cherished keepsake, a sign of better days gone by, or a whimsical flea market find. The cup and the fingers have a tale to tell. As the picture broadens, we draw conclusions and develop opinions based on everything the writer or director chooses to show us.

In this chapter, consider the specific details as described by each writer. Look for treasures in the temperament of each dinner guest. Reflect on each place at the table. Reflect on how the table is set. Consider how these details offer insight into your own dining experience.

WHERE ARE YOU, LITTLE LOST LAMB?

This lesson recounts a dinner party held in honor of a riotous man. Jesus tells this story to a group of indignant men who were complaining about the company that Jesus kept. They were especially concerned that Jesus ate with wicked and dishonest people.

To set the stage, please read Luke 15:11–15.

 Who are the three main characters briefly identified in verse 11?

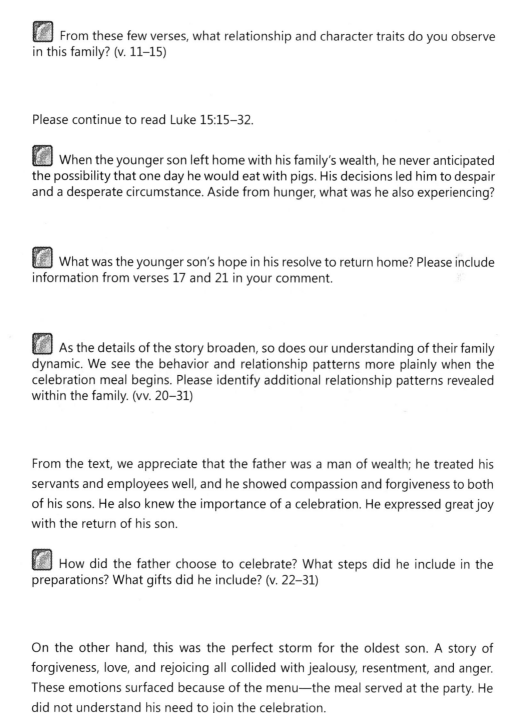

From these few verses, what relationship and character traits do you observe in this family? (v. 11–15)

Please continue to read Luke 15:15–32.

When the younger son left home with his family's wealth, he never anticipated the possibility that one day he would eat with pigs. His decisions led him to despair and a desperate circumstance. Aside from hunger, what was he also experiencing?

What was the younger son's hope in his resolve to return home? Please include information from verses 17 and 21 in your comment.

As the details of the story broaden, so does our understanding of their family dynamic. We see the behavior and relationship patterns more plainly when the celebration meal begins. Please identify additional relationship patterns revealed within the family. (vv. 20–31)

From the text, we appreciate that the father was a man of wealth; he treated his servants and employees well, and he showed compassion and forgiveness to both of his sons. He also knew the importance of a celebration. He expressed great joy with the return of his son.

How did the father choose to celebrate? What steps did he include in the preparations? What gifts did he include? (v. 22–31)

On the other hand, this was the perfect storm for the oldest son. A story of forgiveness, love, and rejoicing all collided with jealousy, resentment, and anger. These emotions surfaced because of the menu—the meal served at the party. He did not understand his need to join the celebration.

▨ What did the older son hear as he approached his home? What was his reaction? (vv. 25–30)

▨ How did he receive a personal invitation to join the party? (v. 28)

Depending on which chair we sit in, we can relate to each of these family members. As we look around the table, we can personally recognize many of the emotions and decisions that were present in this saga. There is always a place for some healing and a little restoration. Yet the father's gentle words—his response to his son's impassioned objection—leave us wondering about the outcome. Perhaps the older son accepted his father's comfort and acknowledged his brother's place in the family. Perhaps that took some time.

Commonly titled *The Prodigal Son*, this story seems to focus on the younger of the two brothers—*prodigal* meaning "wasteful, reckless, or extravagant." It is easy to recognize his fool-hearted behavior and accept his repentance and return home. After all, we all take this path from time to time. The father's gracious welcome and celebration banquet gives us hope and even a longing to be cared for so deeply. Nevertheless, if we take a deeper look and consider the backstory, heaven hopes to serve another very significant—homecoming—meal. Remember, Jesus is telling this story to a group of men who disagreed with his dinner plans.

Please go back a few verses and read Luke 15:1–11.

▨ What is the common issue or problem in these parables? (vv. 4, 8)

▨ What was the cause for rejoicing? (vv. 5, 9)

Who would not look for a lost sheep, and who would not look for a lost coin? These are rhetorical questions, of course, because a responsible person would look for lost property. Relating to modern circumstances, have you ever lost your car keys, or has the dog carried off one of your shoes? Have you left your packages in a restaurant or forgotten where you parked your car? Perhaps a misplaced cell phone or paycheck required a few minutes of your time. The sense of relief and rejoicing when finding even one of these small items helps our understanding of what Jesus was saying.

 Luke 15:7, 10, and 32 tell us the point of the parables. What is it?

There will be rejoicing in heaven in the presence of angels over one sinner who repents. The father in our story rejoiced with the return of his son. He celebrated with a banquet, and music, and dancing. It is fun to wonder what celebrating in heaven might look like and what joy might sound like amongst the angels. However, there is still a little more to the story. While there was great cause for celebrating—because of the younger son's repentant and humbled heart—this part of the story does not follow the pattern of the previous parables. The father was not searching for his younger son.

Recall from the two parables, a man would leave ninety-nine sheep in the wilderness to find one that was missing, and the woman set aside her nine pieces of silver to search in the darkness until she found the lost coin.

 In the story of the prodigal son, who did the father look for? (Luke 15:28)

The father left his youngest son and the banquet guests to find the one person not seated at the table—the one who was with him all along, but refused to celebrate. Aren't you glad the father found him?

For a Bit More to Chew On: The older son declares faithfulness and obedience to his father, yet he had no room in his heart to rejoice with him. How might love change the pattern of his heart? Please consider the words in 1 Corinthians 13:4–7.

Love is patient, love is kind. It does not envy,
it does not boast, it is not proud.
It is not rude, it is not self-seeking, it is not easily
angered, it keeps no record of wrongs. Love does
not delight in evil but rejoices with the truth.
It always protects, always trusts, always hopes, always perseveres.
—1 Corinthians 13:4–7 (NIV)

THE KITCHEN SINK—I FOUND IT

Consider those who sit at your table. Realize that every person—from the youngest to the oldest—is essentially a guest and a visitor on your banquet stage. Each one comes with a backstory; some stories we know, and some we do not. Some of the patterns you share are good, and some you may want to discard. Whether you are a parent, sibling, relative, or friend, you know and experience the daily emotions of those who eat meals with you.

 With this in mind, find a cause to celebrate. Prepare an expression of celebration for your table. For example, display a vase of flowers, light a candle, or place a plate of cookies on the table for dessert. Use your imagination, and pray for inspiration. Consider whether it takes a bit of repentance to carry out this task, or if joy is an expression of your love.

Table Notes:

PART 2: INTRO QUESTION

 Have you ever been left out or unwelcomed at a meal? Briefly explain.

THE EMPTY CHAIR

In this lesson, we will highlight a few dinners of a very prominent character in the Bible. Interestingly, he is known for numerous, notable meals and venues. However, we will focus on the empty chairs at a few of these events and the stories behind the people in the chairs. First, let us get to know a bit about the characters.

The main character in our lesson is David, the youngest son of Jesse. The opening scene takes place in Bethlehem, during a time when Israel was at war with neighboring tribes. Saul, the first king of Israel, had disobeyed God in battle, and while he remained in leadership for some time—in the spiritual sense—he had lost his throne. For this reason, the prophet Samuel set out to anoint a new king. On his quest, Samuel took a heifer to sacrifice to the Lord, and he invited Jesse and Jesse's sons to eat the sacrificial meal.

Please read 1 Samuel 16:1–14.

 What does 1 Samuel 16:7 tell us about the nature of God and man?

At first, Jesse did not include David in this rare and special opportunity for his family: to eat a sacrifice meal with the prophet. Samuel had to insist that David attend.

 What did Samuel say about David's presence at the table? (1 Samuel 16:11b)

What did Samuel do after David arrived? (vv. 12–13)

Please include information from 1 Samuel 16:1 in your answer.

David's brothers watched as Samuel chose David over them. Samuel anointed David to be the king of Israel. What else happened to David in this setting? (v. 13)

What happened to Saul, the king of Israel? (v. 14)

David continued to shepherd his father's sheep while three of his brothers followed Saul into battle against the Philistines. At the request of his father, David traveled to the battlefield with food for his brothers. There he found King Saul and the entire Israeli army very afraid— afraid because of the Philistine champion, Goliath.

Please take a few minutes to read a little more about their family dynamic and David's contrary behavior. As you read, consider how the brothers might convey their story at the family dinner table. Consider how the perspective would change in David's account. Most of the details are character driven, and it would be hard to leave anything out. The information is important to the teller, as he replays the events in his mind and in his heart. Ultimately, the story shows us the character of young David and how his life changed by delivering a meal.

Please read 1 Samuel 17.

From this encounter, what additional insight do you gain about David and his family relationships? (vv. 11–16, 28, 29)

How does David respond to his brothers? (vv. 17:29–30)

▨ Briefly, describe David's courage and faith. (vv. 17:32–37, 45)

▨ From what you have read in this lesson, how would you describe David's brothers?

If you thought it unfair to draw a circumstantial conclusion about the brothers based on these few verses, perhaps you are right. However, we can see from this story that David was familiar with conflict. Challenges with wild animals and with his family had become a backstory to David's character. His chair was empty at the sacrifice meal with Samuel, and he was not welcome when he brought food to his brothers on the battlefield. We also see how he trusted God when challenged.

You may wonder how any of this relates to our dining room. How does David's story relate to the people at our table? Of course, you may recognize Goliath, the big, gnarly character who shows up from time to time—and perhaps the sibling uprisings are no surprise. However, in this story, we get a glimpse of the spiritual component behind conflict—a component that every table knows.

▨ Please read again 1 Samuel 16:13–14. What are the two spiritual personalities present in the lives of David and Saul?

▨ With this in mind, what two spiritual personalities are waging war in the lives of David and Goliath? (1 Samuel 17:43–45)

Once again, we return to the impact of Eden's garden fruit and the knowledge of good and evil. Fear of Goliath and the fear of the worst confronted Israel—fear challenged the people of the living God. Fear had captured the hearts of Saul and his army; fear captured the hearts of David's brothers. They had forgotten to remember their God, they had forgotten to be very strong and courageous, and they had forgotten faith.

 What was the key to victory? (1 Samuel 17:47)

The battle is the Lord's— the ultimate victory cry. The battle at our table is real, and the spiritual component to every battle is real. The opportunity, on our part, is to recognize the opposition for what it is and to remember where our victory comes from. David's battle was not with his brothers, but with their fear. The spirit of fear is our spiritual foe—the adversary, the enemy of faith.

 How did this battle end for the enemy of God? (1 Samuel 17:50 –51)

 What did David want his family to know? (1 Samuel 17:46–47)

I tell you the truth, if you have faith as small as a mustard seed, you can say to this
mountain, 'Move from here to there,' and it will move.
Nothing will be impossible for you.
—Matthew 17:20 (NIV)

THE KITCHEN SINK—MIX IT UP

Sometimes it is obvious the characters around our table do not mix; they are like vinegar and oil. No matter what the circumstance, a pattern of offense challenges the peace. Views, personalities, mannerisms, and backgrounds seem to have no neutral ground. Yet even vinegar and oil will mix with the addition of the right ingredient. The key is using a tested recipe.

Vinegar, which is water-based, and oil do not mix because their surface structures are different. Honey, mustard, and egg yolks have a common surface to both vinegar and oil. In chemical terms, they are surfactants. When you add a surfactant to vinegar and oil, it places itself between the two ingredients and stabilizes the mixture. The stabilized mixture becomes an emulsion. The additional ingredient is necessary to create a bond.

Observe what happens when vinegar and oil are mixed. In a clear glass container, mix 2 tablespoons of edible oil with 2 tablespoons of vinegar. Stir the ingredients until they are completely mixed. Watch to see what happens when the stirring stops. Note what you observe after a few minutes.

Now add 1 teaspoon of mustard, honey, or egg yolk to the vinegar and oil mixture. Stir or whisk it for 30 seconds to create an emulsion. Add salt and pepper for a tasty dressing.

A surfactant reduces the surface tension of vinegar and becomes the bonding agent with oil; it covers the surface of the dissimilar ingredients. With this in mind, what might reduce surface tension between the people at your table? Does it seem impossible?

Please read Matthew 17:20. What two surfactants in this passage lead to amazing possibilities? One is spiritual, and one is physical.

A surfactant reduces surface tension by covering the differences in character. By faith (as small as a *mustard* seed), consider how the application of love might reduce the surface tension at our tables. Sometimes it takes faith to add love. Sometimes we have to look for the right serving spoon. You may be in the experimental stage, but this is a great recipe. Remember, only a very small amount of faith is necessary.

 Please write 1 Peter 4:8.

Part 3: Intro Question

 When was the last time you lingered at the table? Was there an unexpected blessing of favor?

The Flavor of a Favor Luncheon

How would you describe favor? Think for a moment about being favored at work, or in school, or perhaps by a grandparent. Favor may come in the way of praise, attention, or respect. Sometimes it comes with special gifts or tokens of indulgence. It does not take much thought to imagine the contrary reaction of others. Favor seems to come with a price. It did for Joseph, the main character in our story. Before we see how favor played a role at his family table, consider the complex experience of favor in Joseph's life.

 Let us begin with Joseph's youth. We will touch on the highlights, but for the sake of clarity, we will fill in some of the linking details. First, use a dictionary to define *favor*.

Please note: Joseph's father, Jacob, had previously experienced an intense encounter with God, which resulted in a blessing (Genesis 32). During this encounter, God changed Jacob's name to Israel—meaning "God Prevails." Both names, Jacob and Israel, refer to the father of the twelve brothers in this story and their generations. Their families became the nation of Israel, also called the children of Israel, Jews, and Hebrews.

Please read Genesis 37:1–11.

 How did Jacob express favor toward his son, Joseph? (v. 3)

What reaction did Joseph's brothers have as they witnessed this favor? (v. 4)

Further complicating the family dynamic, Joseph had two prophetic dreams. He dreamt that his brothers would one-day bow down to him. Of course, Joseph told them about his dreams, as any seventeen-year old boy would. This only deepened their contempt for Joseph (Genesis 37: 5–11). As the story broadens, consider how divine favor served Joseph with a few bewildering side dishes.

Please read Genesis 37:11–28.

The Lord gave Joseph dreams; they foretold of a divine purpose in Joseph's life. What did Joseph experience that seems a bit contrary to his dreams?

Joseph was loved by his father and was sold into slavery by his brothers. For most, this would be enough family offense to ruin any future relationship—end of story. However, this was just the appetizer. Consider the strange contrast as described in Genesis 39. What would it take to forgive this wrong?

Please read Genesis 39.

Joseph found favor with God and man. What was the evidence of their favor in Genesis 39:1–6?

Potiphar's wife also favored Joseph. What was the result of her attention? (Genesis 39:20)

How was God's favor still apparent while Joseph was in prison? (Genesis 39:21–23)

The Table and Chairs

The pattern of *favor–offense–favor* repeats in each dramatic account of Joseph's life. Many years later, Joseph once again plays a highly favored role, elevated by the favor of God and man. Genesis 41 details events that led him to become the second most powerful man in Egypt.

Please read Genesis 41:41–42:1.

 Please note details that stand out to you.

Please read Genesis 43:16–34, the luncheon story. The *men* in the text are Joseph's brothers.

 Joseph knew these men were his brothers, and he invited them to a meal at noon. Why might you plan a midday meal for out-of-town guests?

This was the second year into the famine, and more than twenty years since Joseph lost the relationship of his family. His brothers had come for food once before, but without Benjamin. At that time, Joseph purposely concealed his kinship, and he spoke to them through an interpreter. On this second occasion, he was dressed as an Egyptian ruler. They still did not know who he was.

 What might cause you to conceal your identity while speaking to people from your past?

As we continue to watch the family at Joseph's table, ponder the backstory to your own table and chairs. Consider the time that has passed with some heartaches unresolved. As we conclude, consider how the lingering effect of favor is evident in the healing of broken relationships.

After twenty years, Joseph wondered if his father—the one who loved him—was still alive. Considering the time that had passed and the heartache he had suffered, describe Joseph's emotion when he saw his younger brother, Benjamin. (Genesis 43:29–31)

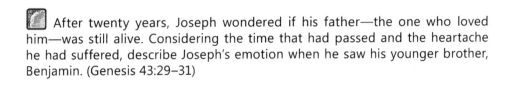 Joseph had a meal prepared, and seated his brothers according to their age. He did not place his chair with theirs—his chair was missing from the family table. But why? How might eleven chairs, representing a family of twelve brothers, stir the hearts of each member?

 How did Joseph express favor to his brother, Benjamin? (v. 34)

Personal Comment:

After the meal, Joseph sent his brothers to their home in Canaan, with the food they had come to purchase. However, the final course waited for their return. Later the same day, Joseph sent again for his brothers by way of a planned conspiracy (Genesis 44:1–14). It was during this third encounter that Joseph was compelled to make himself known.

To conclude, please read Genesis 45:1–15.

How did Joseph embrace his brothers? (Genesis 45:14–15)

How would you summarize God's plan for good that involved tears, an empty chair, and favor at the family table? (Genesis 45:7–10)

The Table and Chairs

The story in this lesson circled all around food. It was about food's impact on a family and their decision to relocate to a new home in Egypt. Strangely, a famine is the meal ticket for their journey. At the end of the journey, a luncheon secured their future. Specifically, it was their place at the table. Beyond that, this reunited family became the most prominent family in all of history. Joseph's dreams represented God's plan to move the entire family, every brother, to the land of Goshen, the place where God would make himself known.

Joseph sums up his experience in Genesis 50:20, where once again those two little words, *good* and *evil*, tell the tale. Joseph responds to his brothers:

> But as for you, ye thought evil against me;
> but God meant it unto good, to bring to pass,
> as *it is* this day, to save much people alive.
> —Genesis 50:20 (KJV)

THE KITCHEN SINK—TIME TELLS ALL

Joseph revealed himself and God's purpose in bits and pieces. Little clues, over time, would compel his family to believe. Slowly he exposed his relationship to them, allowing himself to gradually deal with emotions and manage his reactions. The layering of information also allowed the prophetic nature of his dreams to be proved—unchallenged. When Joseph's brothers bowed down to him, they experienced the hand of God.

Perhaps we can remember this lesson with the tasty message of tapas. Tapas are little appetizers served to promote conversation and encourage a lingering atmosphere. They are bite-sized servings that keep us satisfied and yet wanting a little more.

 Prepare and serve a tapas-style meal, and watch the conversation patterns. Either serve the meal as several small courses, or set the table with small plates, to prolong the time spent together. Note any differences that you may observe. Consider what may be lingering in the hearts of those you dine with, lingering thoughts that need time to tell.

 List a few menu ideas.

 Will there be a need to explain why the meal is different?

 What strategy might you use in order to make the meal successful?

PART 4: INTRO QUESTION

▓ Recall a time when you ventured away from a family meal tradition. Did it feel strange, like something was missing?

We love tradition, don't we? Tradition offers a bit of normal, even if normal feels chaotic or hectic. Meal traditions include gathering for holidays or special occasions. Common customs revolve around the daily routine of a family meal. Traditions also include cultural practices, like table manners, that can leave us wondering what is acceptable in certain circumstances. Simple decisions sometimes seem complicated—like should we talk politics at the table or eat fried chicken with our fingers? Some traditions, embedded in our social structure, pretend to be rules with consequences. Such is the case for a few men in today's story. They were captive to their religious tradition and some cumbersome rules. Ironically, these religious traditions led them so close to the truth, they could taste it, but they considered the ritual of washing their hands more important. Let us see what they were missing.

THE MARKETPLACE

Please read Mark 7:1–5.

▓ Who was eating in these verses? Who was nearby, watching?

▓ What question did the Pharisees ask Jesus? (v. 5)

*The Pharisees and all the Jews do not eat
unless they give their hands a ceremonial washing ...*
—Mark 7:3 (NIV)

It seems amazing that the tradition of hand washing before a meal came with such deep religious undertones. The ritual went far beyond personal hygiene; it was ceremonial, and it warranted a narrative in the Bible. However, while the history of hand washing is extensive, our focus will be on what the Pharisees missed when their gaze could see nothing else. The question is if all Jews washed their hands before eating, why did the disciples—who were definitely Jews—abandon what was a very common and even habitual practice before this meal? They neglected a practice so embedded in the culture that ignoring it drew scrutiny and disgust. What backstory did the disciples bring to the table that day? What eclipsed tradition? Once again, let us look into the venue and the recent circumstances. Once again, consider why the people at your table may also challenge the status-quo.

 Mark 7:4 gives us a clue about the venue. Where does the story take place?

The disciples had either come from the marketplace or dined near the marketplace, a public venue where the Pharisees could easily observe. The marketplace—perceived as an unclean place and populated by unclean people—naturally drew crowds and activity. However, something different was happening, something new, something out of the ordinary. To see what was brewing, please read a few of the previous verses in Mark 6.

Please read Mark 6:53–7:2.

 When the disciples anchored their boat at Gennesaret and when the people recognized Jesus, what immediately happened?

The disciples saw people running to see Jesus. They were coming from everywhere; they even laid sick people in the street in hopes that Jesus would heal them. Did the overflow of attention toward Jesus and the energy of the crowds cause the disciples to have a lack of judgment? Were they just tired of all the rules? Perhaps and quite possibly, other ingredients went into this non-traditional meal—the meal eaten with unwashed hands.

Please continue to read a little further back. Please read Mark 6:34–53.

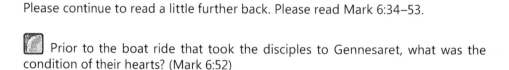 Prior to the boat ride that took the disciples to Gennesaret, what was the condition of their hearts? (Mark 6:52)

 What miracle had they not considered? (Mark 6: 52)

We're not there yet. Let us take a deeper look into that boat ride. Something had a major impact on the disciples—something more than feeding thousands of people with a few loaves of bread and some fish. The same story, in Matthew, includes a few more details.

Please read Matthew 14:19–34.

 What did Peter do when he crawled out of the boat? (Matthew 14:29)

 Comment on what became clear to the disciples during the boat ride. (Matthew 14:33)

Imagine the wind and the water pounding your face. Imagine the weariness of struggling against the waves and the darkness of the night. Imagine seeing what you thought was a ghost. Imagine recognizing the Son of God. Imagine Jesus, dressed in humanity, the King of Kings, the Lord of Lords, and the celebrated Prince of Heaven, walking toward you, calming the seas in your life.

Personal Observation:

Then imagine neglecting to wash your hands. These experiences came with the disciples to the table. Imagine having a conversation with them. Imagine what the Pharisees missed by watching rather than eating lunch with them.

The disciples, their backstory, their accusers, and Jesus were all present at the table. They each embraced the moment, but their perspectives were not the same, nor were their actions.

Please read Matthew 15:10–20.

What did Jesus say about the tradition of washing hands? (Matthew 15:11 and 20)

How did the Pharisees react to words Jesus spoke to the crowd? (Matthew 15:12)

How did Jesus instruct the disciples concerning the Pharisees? (Matthew 15:14)

Please read Romans 10:8–10.

For a Bit More to Chew On: Jesus spoke to the crowds about his Word and our words. How do the words that come from our mouths and our hearts reflect our faith?

A cheerful heart is good medicine,
but a crushed spirit dries up the bones.
—Proverbs 17:22 (NIV)

THE KITCHEN SINK—IMAGINE CHANGE

Today's view into the backstory of the disciples is an example of how daily encounters have their impact at the table. Of course, the Pharisees had a backstory too. Their backstory held them in a pattern that was rigid and unforgiving; they did not understand or refused to see the need for change. To help us consider how the patterns in our lives may need a second look, make a table setting alteration. Set your table in an unusual way. For example, serve salad in a teacup or set the table with the dinner plate turned upside down. Use your imagination— remember each chair and each place setting holds an active and evolving story.

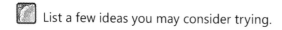 List a few ideas you may consider trying.

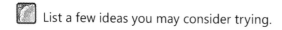 Note the reactions and insights you gain from this shift of routine, this slight pattern alteration.

PART 5: INTRO QUESTION

 Recall a time when you ate with unfamiliar people at a family table. How did the unusual company make you feel?

The meal stories in the Old and New Testament all center on one family and one nation—God's chosen people of Israel—until the New Testament book of Acts. In the book of Acts, the food on the table changes, as do the people. The meals begin to include all the peoples of the world, and the strict dietary laws of Moses relax to include some quite unexpected ingredients. This was a challenging concept for the Jewish community. Peter, the man who walked on water with Jesus, and who ate without washing his hands, announces this incredible pattern shift. His personal encounters with Jesus give him credibility as he takes tradition off the table and writes a new family menu—a recipe of good news.

CRAB CAKES AND BACON

Our lesson opens with four main characters, Cornelius, Peter, an angel, and a voice. Cornelius is an Italian officer in the Roman army—importantly, he is not Jewish. Peter, on the other hand, is a Jew and a follower of Jesus; he is also one of the twelve apostles. The angel and the voice are from heaven. The story takes place in two different venues, with two different messages from God. Each message is retold several times. As you read, consider the retelling of these events from your personal perspective—had you been there, had you talked with an angel, had you seen a vision that would touch the world.

Please read Acts 10:1–20.

 What do you learn about Cornelius from these verses? (vv. 1–8)

What did Cornelius tell his servants? (vv. 7–8)

If your boss told you, "I talked with an angel," what would you think?

What was Peter thinking about when he fell into a trance? (v. 10)

Briefly describe what Peter saw coming down from heaven. (Acts 10:11 and 12)

Peter saw, as commonly described, a tablecloth filled with unclean animals, reptiles, and birds—forbidden food according to the Mosaic (Jewish) Law. While our study is themed around food, our discussion about clean and unclean food will be limited to a few basics. However, the topic does relate to us and to the people at our table. It was also extremely important to Peter and the people who ate with him.

Leviticus 11 describes the unclean and forbidden food as defined by Moses. These regulations were for Israel, the Jewish nation. It only takes a few verses to get a sense of their restricted diet.

Please read from the third book in the Bible, Leviticus 11:1–27.
(Read the entire chapter for the complete list.)

Compare the differences between this list and the forbidden food mentioned in Genesis 2:16–17. Briefly note new insight you gain from these two passages.

Which is easier, to eat from every tree except one or to deny yourself lobster and bacon? Do you wonder what changed? Do you wonder why this much longer list of forbidden food became part of the Jewish law? Then, did you notice the *no touching* clause (Leviticus 11:24–27)? Does it remind you of the serpent's conversation with

Eve in the Garden (Genesis 3)? Peter knew the stories, and he understood the law—hence the troubling nature of his vision.

What did the voice say in Acts 10:13?

What did the voice say the second time? (Acts 10:15)

What was Peter's response? (Acts 10:14)

Perplexed by this vision and the message of the voice, Peter had little time to negotiate his thoughts. The men sent by Cornelius had arrived; these men were Gentiles and considered unclean.

> Character notes for the next part of the story: By Jewish reference, anyone not a Jew was a Gentile; a distinguishing difference was circumcision. Circumcision marked a covenant with God—a contract in the flesh. Most Jewish males were circumcised as babies; Gentiles were not. Amongst Jews, they called themselves the circumcised. Jews called Gentiles the uncircumcised. Circumcised believers were Jewish men who believed in Jesus as their Savior. Gentiles who believed in Jesus were identified as Christians.

Please continue to read Acts 10:20–48.

Which Jewish custom did Peter's vision challenge? (Acts 10:28)

How did Peter's vision also apply to Gentiles? (Acts: 10:34–35)

For Peter, this was on-the-job training—something he was familiar with, and something experience had taught him to accept. As he traveled with the men up the Mediterranean coastline, he had time to pray and ponder the reason for his trip to Caesarea. He had time to cast down the argument that undoubtedly came to his mind. He had time to rehearse the word spoken to him, "Go with them, doubting nothing: for I have sent them" (Acts 10:20 KJV).

After the introductions, what did Peter ask? (Acts 10:29)

How did Cornelius respond in the second half of verse 33?

With what evidence did Peter express his undeniable knowledge of the resurrected Jesus? (Acts 10:41)

Please continue to read Acts 11:1–18.

Explain why men criticized Peter in Acts 11:3.

Do you find it surprising that eating a meal with someone could have such broad implications? The news of Peter's meal companions traveled from Caesarea to Jerusalem, from apostles to friends. Yet it was the plan of God to introduce the Gentile nations into his kingdom by way of a controversial meal. It got people talking. It got people listening. The story of people eating a meal together caused them to believe.

What were some results of Peter's conversation with Cornelius? (Acts 11: 15–18)

> For there is no difference between Jew and Gentile—the same
> Lord is Lord of all and richly blesses all who call on him, for,
> "Everyone who calls on the name of the Lord will be saved."
> —Romans 10:12–13 (NIV)

THE KITCHEN SINK—SHINE AND SPARKLE

Have you ever spoken to an angel or heard a voice from heaven? How might you repeat that story? Would there be passion in your voice, with a sense of excitement or determined purpose? Would you have a quiet resolve for a hard-to-explain experience of supernatural truth? Might you tell the story one time and then once again? The story of Peter's vision and the meaning of the vision communicated a pivotal pattern change in the clean/unclean conversation. It not only changed the Jewish rules about food; this marked a crucial difference in those invited to the table. Cornelius, a chosen Gentile, spoke with an angel who compelled him to find the truth. As a result, he sat and had a meal with Peter, and talked first-hand with a man who knew Jesus.

Is God speaking to you about a relationship that needs a new pattern? Are you holding on to a principle that justifies your position? Briefly note the principle that reinforces your position.

Choose something in your kitchen that needs a little cleaning—some sparkle and shine. Choose a project that you can finish in ten or fifteen minutes. As you work, have a conversation with God about your position in the relationship mentioned above. Ask him to clean and polish your position. Be prepared; you may need to yield to a new perspective.

Briefly note your experience.

Please review the next page to prepare for the Group Taste-and-See Experience.

Group Taste-and-See Experience

TASTY BITES: APPETIZERS

Appetizers are little treats before dinner. The type of appetizer can reflect the type of food served for the main meal, such as chips and salsa before a Mexican meal, or salami and cheese before an Italian meal. Of course, a few slices of fruit or a bowl of mixed nuts served before a meal equally satisfies.

Traditionally, the purpose of appetizers is to gather those in from a busy day to relax and prepare for a meal—to calm ravenous appetites awaiting the final meal preparations. Appetizers help set the stage for an enjoyable time together.

Prepare an appetizer for the group to share. Choose a favorite or try something new. Display bite-size servings on a dish or platter. For this exercise, take a few minutes to garnish the dish with a flower or edible greenery. Remember, this is practice for many who have never prepared such a dish.

DISCUSSION SUGGESTIONS

- Discuss the presentation—the colors, textures, and flavors of individual appetizer dishes. Discuss when simple dishes, such as a slice of fruit, may be a perfect complement to a meal.
- When is a more substantial bite most appropriate?
- How might appetizers improve the atmosphere of your family's meal?
- Discuss how weather, the time of day, and the people at your table might determine the types of appetizers you serve; i.e. Cheerios might be a great appetizer for toddlers.
- Discuss where to serve appetizers—at the table or not.

As you know, dinner conversations are more than words that linger in air. They are words that contain a backstory and relationship, however slight or intense the relationship may be. These conversations often shape our lives and direct our focus. How important is it then to pay thoughtful attention to the dialogue and, like in any good recipe, add a little salt when necessary.

We most often think of conversations between people, but in this chapter, we will include the conversations we have with God. If you think about it, every conversation in the Bible includes the voice of God. Each story recites his Word.

Let your conversation be always full of grace, seasoned with salt,
so that you may know how to answer everyone.
—Colossians 4:6 (NIV)

The Conversation

- Objective: To know God participates in conversation.
- Bible Topic: Conversation leads to relationship.
- Bible Food: Salt
- Food Topic: Meat
- Food to be Prepared: Soup or Stew

PART 1: INTO QUESTION

 What is your favorite way to hear that dinner is ready?

BETWEEN A ROCK AND A HARD PLACE

"Dinner is ready"—a simple call to the table and expressed a thousand ways—circles the broad scope of conversation style. The tone and expression of our words lend flavor to the dialogue. The tone can sound bitter or sweet, sour or spicy, and the expression might feel somewhere between gritty and smooth. In today's story, a conversation between a man and his donkey reveals the hidden component in many conversations—a reason for the tone and the intention behind the attitude. A deeper look exposes something that most often goes unexplained. At first, the donkey is a silent communicator, but when she does finally speak, her words include an intriguing spiritual insight. As you read, consider what we might see in the silence. Also, consider the very physical evidence of God's intent to direct the narrative.

Please read Numbers 22:20–38.

 List the characters that have speaking parts in this fantastic account.

 Briefly note what you find remarkable, interesting, or thought-provoking in these conversations.

So who is Balaam? How is it that he had a one-on-one with God? How is it that he had a one-on-one with his donkey? His conversations, like all others, do have a backstory. Sensationally, his donkey had a backstory too. While these are not meal conversations, there is a lot to digest.

Balaam's story begins in Numbers 22:5. He was a man with dangerous power and familiarity. His reputation and influence reached generations throughout the Bible. His occupation generated this notorious fame.

Please read Numbers 22:1–12.

 What was the occupation of Balaam? (Numbers 22:7)

Divination, like witchcraft, is the attempt to gain insight and influence by way of occult ritual and practices. Kings hired Balaam to use this practice to curse their enemies. Balaam had gained notoriety—his evil practice proven. He was the expert, he was well versed in cursing man, and he was rewarded with wealth for doing so.

Please reread Numbers 22:1–12.

 In response to Balak's request, what did Balaam say to the elders of Moab and Midian? (v. 8)

 How did God open the dialogue with Balaam? (v. 9)

 From their conversation, what did God tell Balaam in verse 12?

But God said to Balaam, "Do not go with them. You must not put a curse on those people, because they are blessed!"
—Numbers 22:12 (NIV)

The Conversation

Please recall what you remember about these blessed people. They had been slaves in Egypt and then led to freedom at the hand of Moses. They were the children who stayed indoors during the first Passover, dressed and ready to go. They were the families who heard the Egyptian cries that night, and they fled with Egyptian riches. God delivered them in an awesome display, and he blessed them. Now they were on a journey through the wilderness, to the Promised Land. Their numbers, their victories, and their God brought fear to Moab and other kings. In their fear, Balak sought Balaam to curse the children of Israel.

God said to Balaam, "Don't go ..."

Please continue to read Numbers 22:13–22.

At first, Balaam yielded to God's command. He told Balak's officials to go home. How did Balaam respond to the next group of distinguished officials, men who offered him riches and prestige? (v. 18)

Have you ever asked God for direction and kept asking until you got the answer that you wanted? What did Balaam do in verse 21?

This information gives a broader insight into Balaam's character. A conversation with Balaam might have been menacing and perilous, but he did know God, and God knew him. This passage also allows us insight to God's character. The significance, of course, is God's participation in the dialogue. He provided a voice to the narrative; he protected the blessing of Israel.

Please read again about Balaam and his talking donkey in Numbers 22:20–35.

What were the donkey's first words? (v. 28)

What was it that Balaam did not see? (v. 22)

God opened the donkey's mouth, and then he opened Balaam's eyes. Picture a conversation with Balaam as he rehearsed the details of his journey—as he described the anger that he felt when his donkey disobeyed. Imagine his emotions as he described the angel of the Lord. Did everyone grow silent—did their attention heightened? Imagine their focus as he spoke words like these: *"After the donkey quit speaking to me, the angel of the LORD told me to go."*

His donkey, on the other hand, might bray out a different version. She knew the dark skills of the man she was talking with. She also knew that there was the angel of the Lord, with a sword, standing in front of her. Perhaps we can learn something from the donkey's choice of words.

 What did the donkey say in verse 30?

By nature, donkeys have a stubborn and relentless sense of self-preservation. The donkey in our story endured the cruelty of her master as she faced the opposing sword of an angel. Who was more dangerous? One might suppose that her words would be aggressive, defensive, or hostile. Instead, we see the nature of God in her words and the able potency to turn away wrath. Proverbs 15:1 mirrors this scenario. Do you suppose the power behind the proverb lies in the unseen realm?

 Please write Proverbs 15:1.

Balaam had a significant relationship with God, even though his ways were perverse. He had real conversations with God, and God spoke to him about his words. One might wonder how to know the voice of God—how you might distinguish God's words from your own. James 3:17 lends us a clue to knowing God's voice—wisdom from above.

The Conversation

Please read James 3:17–18.

 What qualities of character come with wisdom from above? Does wisdom from above align with what you know to be good?

An interesting final note is Balaam's use of food. Balaam used food, like that serpent of old, to cause men to stumble, and his practices continued to have an effect on the generations that followed.

Please read from the last book in the Bible, Revelation 2:14.

 How did the doctrine of Balaam cause Israel to stumble?

It is hard to envision the stories that deserved such repute. However, God continued to be keenly involved with Balaam's endeavors and present in his conversations.

Because they met not the children of Israel with bread and with water,
but hired Balaam against them, that he should curse them:
howbeit our God turned the curse into a blessing.
—Nehemiah 13:2 (KJV)

THE KITCHEN SINK—SHAKE IT UP

Balaam questioned his donkey's behavior, not seeing the entire picture. Dinner conversations quite often leave us with questions as well. We have to wait for days, weeks, or even years to understand the meaning behind someone's tears, or passion, or tenacious animosity. The picture is more completely revealed as we come to understand the backstories. Our backstories include plans and roadblocks to plans. Backstories affect the way we listen and the way we interact. How useful it is to ask the questions. How useful it is to know that God is listening. How useful it is to know that God is an active participant in our conversations.

> Let your conversation be always full of grace, seasoned with salt,
> so that you may know how to answer everyone.
> —Colossians 4:6 (NIV)

The word *salt*, in Colossians 4:6, means "wisdom and grace exhibited in speech" (*Strong's* halas, #217). Below are a few characteristics of salt. When you consider that wisdom is the salt of conversation, our words take on a powerful meaning.

- Salt suppresses bitterness and enriches the flavor of food.
- Salt is a preservative.
- Salt is necessary for life.
- Salt is not an herb or a spice.
- Salt dissolves and physically changes the molecular structure of the substance it mixes with.

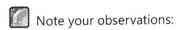 Consider salt as a way of allowing God to season the narrative and perhaps the dialogue. As visual reminders, place several saltshakers or containers of salt around your home. Listen to your conversations and consider the properties of salt, as described above. Identify the flavor of your words in the conversation. Remember, in the story of Balaam, God's conversation flavor was to bless.

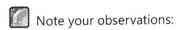 Note your observations:

PART 2: INTRO QUESTION

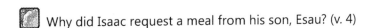 Have you ever been involved in a family feud? Do you know how it started? Briefly explain.

DINNER AND A BLESSING

The scenario in this lesson is a perfect example of how a family feud might begin. There is always a little backstory to fuel the fire, but the conversation stirs the proverbial pot. On the other hand, it is a story about choice. Let us see how this planned choice had you in mind.

The story involves a family: Isaac, his wife Rebekah, and their twin sons, Jacob and Esau. As you read, recognize how this officially God-chosen family is not immune from errors in judgment or even some identity fraud. Recognize how each son passionately wrestles for the blessing of his father.

Please read Genesis 27:1–25.

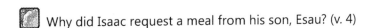 Why did Isaac request a meal from his son, Esau? (v. 4)

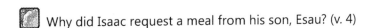 What did Rebekah request from Jacob and why? (vv. 9–10)

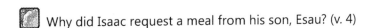 What was Jacob's concern? (vv. 11–12)

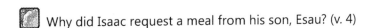 What do you find thought-provoking about Rebekah's strategy? (vv. 11–17)

Did you notice that the narrative does not include the motive behind Rebekah's plan? She accepts the responsibility for her actions; however, she is determined that the blessing be given to Jacob. Before we rush to judgment, perhaps some history will reveal how this meal comes into play.

Please read Genesis 25:19–26

 How long did Rebekah wait for a child? (vv. 20, 26)

 What did the Lord speak to Rebekah about her children during her pregnancy?

With this thought in mind, please read the rest of our meal story. Please read Genesis 27:18–43.

 What question did Isaac ask Jacob in Genesis 27:18?

 What prevented Isaac from recognizing his son, Jacob? (Genesis 27:1, 21–27)

Do your emotions get all over this story? Do you read between the lines and take sides? Have you ever plotted like Rebekah or trembled like Isaac? Have you ever raised your voice like Esau, with a great and exceedingly bitter cry? Then again, have you ever fled for your life?

The passion was real, and the drama was intense. An ache and raw upheaval engaged the heart of each family member. Moreover, the family turmoil begins over a meal—some savory meat, a piece of bread, and a cup of wine.

Well, we know there is more to this meal. The blessing, of course, was key—a conversation that included prophetic words spoken by faith. The question is, did the conversation change history or confirm history? God had chosen Jacob before he was born. He chose Jacob before he had done good or evil, before Rebekah held him her arms, and before Isaac knew his name. God chose Jacob before Esau became a hunter, before Esau walked or spoke a word. With the choice came a blessing.

After Isaac ate, he blessed his younger son, Jacob. What was the blessing? (Genesis 27:28–29)

What was Esau's blessing? (vv. 39–40)

What caused the family feud? (v. 41)

We can remember the story of Jacob and Esau by the meal of savory food. The feud lasted for twenty years, until Jacob humbly returned with his eleven sons and their mothers. Jacob experienced, many times, the pain of deceit as he wrestled to rebuild his life. Nevertheless, the blessing remained. Confirming evidence of the blessing occurred in a most unusual way. This time there was no identity fraud.

Please read Genesis 32:22–32

What question was Jacob asked in Genesis 32:27?

What was the result of the struggle?

Jacob became Israel, a man who wrestled with God. Through his lineage came Jesus. With Jesus comes another conversation. It is a conversation just as passionate and just as intense. This conversation also includes a blessing. Opposition to this blessing also comes with an exceeding and bitter cry.

The Conversation

Paul explains the blessing in a letter to the Ephesians.

Please read Ephesians 1:3–4 and 11–14.

 What is the blessing in Ephesians 1:3?

 Please complete this phrase from verse 4.

He chose us before the _____.

 When are we included to receive the blessing? (Ephesians 1:13)

Think about it: the choice belongs to God. He chose Jacob, and he chose us who believe. We are all free to believe, but many do not. Why is there such a struggle? Where does the bitter opposition come from? What is the conversation that causes unbelief?

God chose to bless those who have faith and believe in his son, Jesus. Those who cry in bitter opposition want the blessing, but they want a different plan.

Personal Notes:

Trust in the LORD with all your heart
and lean not on your own understanding;
in all your ways acknowledge him,
and he will make your paths straight.
—Proverbs 3:5–6 (NIV)

THE KITCHEN SINK—A CHOICE CUT

In an ideal kitchen setting, with a perfectly stocked pantry, with every good produce, spice, and cooking ingredient, and with the ultimate amount of time and expertise, how would you choose to prepare a savory meat? Would your choice be ethnic or an old family recipe? Would it be rare or well-done, barbequed, broiled, baked, stewed, or flavored in a savory sauce? It is your choice. What sounds perfectly delicious to you?

What is the motivating factor behind your choice?

What flavor do you anticipate as you think about your choice?

If time and opportunity allows, prepare a meat dish (or meat alternative) to be included in your evening meal. You may choose to prepare it differently than in the exercise above, but it will still be your choice.

Meal notes:

But God hath chosen the foolish things of
the world to confound the wise;
and God hath chosen the weak things of the world
to confound the things which are mighty.
—1 Corinthians 1:27 (KJV)

PART 3: INTRO QUESTION

 What is your favorite conversation topic at the breakfast table and why?

I KNEW YOU'D COME

The meal in today's lesson is breakfast. The venue is on the beach, and the conversation is personal. It takes place soon after the dramatic and very public crucifixion of Jesus, after the three grueling days when Jesus lay in the tomb, and shortly after his resurrection. Peter and the other disciples were wary of Jewish retaliation, and they chose to isolate themselves from the general population. Their experiences together were undeniable, and yet, individually, they faced their own questions and challenges with their faith. On this day, in the early morning, after breakfast, a conversation answered some of these questions.

Please John 21:1–25.

 Who initiated the fishing trip? (v. 3)

 How would you describe Peter's reaction once he realized Jesus was on the shore? (John 21:7)

If you know the history of Peter, also known as Simon or Simon Peter, you know he was impetuous, impulsive, and demonstrative. In this scene, it seems he could no longer just sit around and wait. He announced that he was going fishing—returning to a familiar activity, a venue where he met Jesus and the setting where his life was changed.

Let us take a brief look back to some of Peter's earlier fishing and boating sagas with Jesus. Without knowing this history, this particular breakfast on the beach might seem random or merely convenient for the resurrected Savior; Jesus could have chosen to appear anywhere. However, history allows us to savor the significance of the venue, the meal, and the conversation. Once again, the backstory makes this private meal rich with personal depth.

Please read Luke 5:1–10.

 What did Simon Peter say in Luke 5:5?

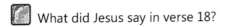 How many fish did Peter catch? (vv. 6–7)

Please read Mark 1:16–18.

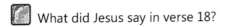 What did Jesus say to Simon Peter in verse 17?

Please read Matthew 14:17–30.

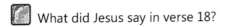 What did Jesus say in verse 18?

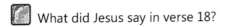 What meal did Simon Peter have before he walked on water?

As John tells the breakfast story, a pattern reveals intimate care. The closeness and awareness of the details enrich the narrative. As a long night of unproductive fishing replays, so does the reward of recasting their nets. With a familiar voice, Jesus beckons them again to bring what they have. He prepares and serves yet another meal of fish and bread. His presence reassures them—it reminds them. They remember what he did and begin to understand all that he had taught.

Breakfast on the beach was the third time Jesus appeared to Peter and the disciples after he rose from the dead; it was the third meal he ate with them as the resurrected King. It makes you wonder why food became such an integral part of each appearance. Why did Jesus want them to know that eating was a part of the resurrected life?

Please read Luke 24:11–33. They heard that the tomb was empty, and they did not believe.

What question did Jesus ask in verse 17?

What were the men doing when they recognized Jesus? (vv. 30–31)

Please continue to read Luke 24:34–35.

What question did Jesus ask in Luke 24:38?

After Jesus ate some broiled fish, what did he do? (Luke 24:45)

The first two meals happened only days after the crucifixion, only days after the Passover meal (the Last Supper), and only days after the earth quaked and light escaped from the afternoon sky. Reeling from the drama and the emotion, the disciples were compelled to evaluate their conviction and their understanding of the truth. They needed to enter a walk of faith. You may wonder why they doubted. If you had journeyed with Jesus and had seen the amazing things he had done, would you believe?

Returning to our breakfast story in John 21, what did the disciples see when they came to land? (John 21:9)

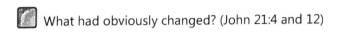 What had obviously changed? (John 21:4 and 12)

How did Jesus greet his disciples? (John 21:12)

What does John 21:14 say?

Something about Jesus was different. The men recognized him by his persona, his mannerisms, and his character patterns that they had grown to know—but something was different. His flesh and bones had changed; his appearance had transformed. They no longer doubted. They believed. Can you imagine how odd, and interesting, and peculiar it all must have seemed? Jesus was waiting for them; he was cooking for them; and then he ate with them, again.

Please reread John 21:15–25.

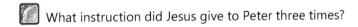 When did Jesus begin his conversation with Peter? (John 21:15)

 What was Peter's response to the *love* questions?

What instruction did Jesus give to Peter three times?

This very significant and intimate conversation with Peter happened after eating a meal together. The conversation included listening and answering questions. It presented hard questions that caused Peter some grief and sadness; the conversation engaged instruction, some direction, and some gentle rebuke.

Jesus instructed Peter, "Feed my lambs; feed my sheep." With these words comes the implication of shepherding and tending the young and old, the mature and immature. Jesus also included some very pointed words for Peter: "*You* must follow me."

For a Bit More to Chew On: How was breakfast on the beach an example for Peter to follow?

And there are also many other things which Jesus did, the which,
if they should be written every one, I suppose that
even the world itself could not contain the books that should be written. Amen.
—John 21:25 (KJV)

THE KITCHEN SINK—SOLID FOOD

For Peter, breakfast on the beach held a welcome visit and a hard conversation. Hebrews 5:13–14 relates that hard topics, like meat, are for the mature, whereas milk is for the young and inexperienced.

Jesus opened his conversation with Peter by asking a simple question: "Do you love me?" It is a simple question and yet profound. These four little words held Peter's backstory, his venerability, his brokenness, and his faith. For some, this question is tough and hard to chew.

For today's exercise, evaluate dinner conversation topics. Many topics may seem simple, such as love, but are actually quite difficult for some, with mysteries held in the guarded regions of their heart. Note several typical conversation topics that you have during meals with others. Then mark if the topic is meat or milk—hard or easy to swallow.

Dinner Conversation Topic	Meat	Milk

Consider the people you speak with at the table. How do these topics meet their *digestive* appetites or palates?

Anyone who lives on milk, being still an infant,
is not acquainted with the teaching about righteousness.
But solid food is for the mature, who by constant use have
trained themselves to distinguish good from evil.
—Hebrews 5:13–14 (NIV)

PART 4: INTRO QUESTION

 Have you ever avoided an uncomfortable conversation? What means of escape did you use?

STIRRING THE POT

Conversations cover many different topics. As we know, some topics are uncomfortable; they challenge our sense of security, and they confront who we are. Sometimes we avoid these conversations at a great price. In this lesson, a dinner guest directly confronts one man's attempt to maneuver himself far from the dialogue. God chose the dinner guest and prepared the meal; he also prepared the strange circumstance and bizarre venue as an atmosphere for listening, contemplation, and a remarkable consequence. The dinner guest was a great fish; Jonah, unwittingly, joined him for a three-day buffet.

Please read Jonah 1:1–17.

What conversation did Jonah try to avoid? (vv. 1– 2)

From whom was Jonah running?

What was the cause of Jonah's distress? (Jonah 1:10)

We do not have a backstory for Jonah, but we can assume a few things from his call to Nineveh. In fact, we can surmise a very common characteristic about every individual that we have studied to this point. God had a very active interest in their lives, their activities, and their conversations.

In Jonah's case, this was not the first time he had heard the voice of God. Jonah did not question the call or wonder if it was really God speaking to him. Tried and tested, Jonah knew God (Jonah 4: 1–3). Like David when he stood before Goliath, Jonah had been prepared—he had experience. Jonah had the faith necessary to preach amidst an evil generation, in an evil city; he had the knowledge and understanding necessary to deliver a powerful message. He simply chose not to.

Please continue to read Jonah 2:1–10.

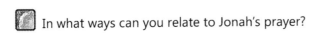 In what ways can you relate to Jonah's prayer?

 How did Jonah season his conversation with God during this three-day experience? (Jonah 2:9)

Figuratively, were you able to place yourself in the sensations of Jonah's ordeal? Did the depths of the sea, with currents and waves and seaweed, remind you of an emotional or physical time of being a fugitive—a runaway from God? Have you had conversations with God that were as serious? Did you stay with the conversation, in prayer, long enough to speak a word of praise and thanksgiving?

Please continue to read Jonah 3:1–10.

 What happened in Jonah 3:1?

 What was the hard conversation that Jonah ultimately entered into with the people of Nineveh? (Jonah 3:4)

Throughout the Old Testament, there are many references to the great city of Nineveh, its kings, and its people. They were not a part of the Jewish nation, but God knew their ways, and on this occasion, their wickedness was no longer tolerable. Their destruction was imminent.

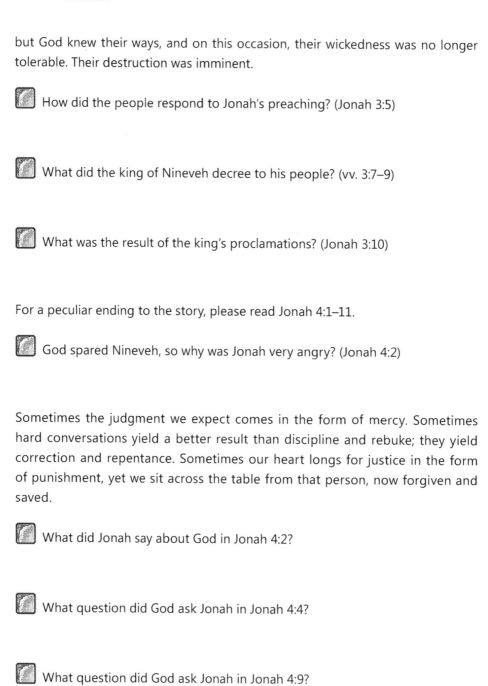 How did the people respond to Jonah's preaching? (Jonah 3:5)

What did the king of Nineveh decree to his people? (vv. 3:7–9)

What was the result of the king's proclamations? (Jonah 3:10)

For a peculiar ending to the story, please read Jonah 4:1–11.

God spared Nineveh, so why was Jonah very angry? (Jonah 4:2)

Sometimes the judgment we expect comes in the form of mercy. Sometimes hard conversations yield a better result than discipline and rebuke; they yield correction and repentance. Sometimes our heart longs for justice in the form of punishment, yet we sit across the table from that person, now forgiven and saved.

What did Jonah say about God in Jonah 4:2?

What question did God ask Jonah in Jonah 4:4?

What question did God ask Jonah in Jonah 4:9?

God prepared a whale for the good of Nineveh. He prepared a gourd and worm for the good of Jonah. Think about it: What was the benefit of the worm?

How does God compare the gourd to the one hundred and twenty thousand people of Nineveh and their cattle?

He hath shewed thee, O man, what is good;
and what doth the LORD require of thee, but to do justly, and to love mercy,
and to walk humbly with thy God?
—Micah 6:8 (KJV)

THE KITCHEN SINK—I HAVE A QUESTION FOR YOU

Have you noticed that God often opens his conversations with a question? This is not to assume he will ask everyone a question. It is, however, a fascinating example of how to begin a dialogue.

God came to Balaam and asked, "Who are these men with you?"

He asked Jacob, "What is your name?"

Jesus asked Peter, "Do you love me?"

The Lord replied to Jonah, "Is it right for you to be angry?"

With certain persons in mind, list a few hard questions you would like answered.

1.

2.

3.

With these questions in mind, list topics that might lead the conversation to a relevant place for asking the question.

1.

2.

3.

For a Bit More to Chew On: What question is God asking you?

Jesus asked him, "What do you want me to do for you?"
—Luke 18:41 (NIV)

PART 5: INTRO QUESTION

 What season of your life do you talk about most often?

IT'S TIME

As we approach the conclusion of our study, it is our hope that you have seen the presence of God in every gift, plan, venue, invitation, meal, and conversation. We hope that each Kitchen Sink exercise has drawn you closer to knowing the goodness of God and tasting his excellent ways.

Solomon conveyed the essence of this experience when he wrote:

> A man can do nothing better than to eat and drink
> and find satisfaction in his work.
> This too, I see, is from the hand of God,
> for without him, who can eat or find enjoyment?
> —Ecclesiastes 2:24–25 (NIV)

In our final meal story, consider how the enjoyment of a meal is a personal decision. Circumstance is relevant, but as we know, matters of the heart change with time. Our conversations lend clues to help us identify the seasons in our lives—times appointed by God for his plan and purpose.

Please read Ecclesiastes 3:1–13. Consider how these appointed times in our lives relate to the conversations we have at the table.

 Which of these verses have a strong link to conversation?

One obvious verse about conversation is Ecclesiastes 3:7b—a time to be silent and a time to speak. However, as you read and reread these verses, it is easy to see how each scenario finds its way into our conversation. Love communicates across the table with a whisper, and hate communicates with no words at all. Laughter and tears interlace emotion between words. An embrace, a dance, or a somber mood each perform and radiate—perhaps simultaneously—from those who dine with us.

So why is this important to know? Why did Solomon take the time to write the obvious? What was his quest; what was his purpose? What had he come to know? Once again, let's look into the backstory of our main character. Consider Solomon's conversation with the Lord as he put on the crown and throne of Israel.

Please read 1 Kings 3:3–15.

What did Solomon request in his dream? How did God respond to his request? (vv. 9–13)

Apparently comforted and delighted with God's answer to his request, how did Solomon celebrate? (v. 15)

With a peculiar wisdom, Solomon wrote about the seasons of life. He wrote about conversation and food and the effort to enjoy. The story of Hannah can perhaps provide a peek into the motivation of Solomon's heart.

Consider the conversations at Hannah's family table. At first, the tale of Hannah is hard to understand. Her story contains the mystery concealed in God's plan. However, if you view her journey from the end of the story, understanding comes with a perspective of hope.

Please read 1 Samuel 1:1–20.

Who taunted Hannah at the table, year after year?

What did Hannah observe at the table—what deepened her anguish year after year? Consider the clues in verses 2 and 4.

How did Hannah's husband treat her? (v. 5)

What did Hannah's husband say that did little to console her? (v. 8)

Where did these dinners take place? (v. 9)

Personal Observation:

Childless, Hannah watched year after year as new babies arrived in her rival's arms. She listened year after year to provoking words—words that caused her anguish and bitter tears. Year after year, her husband's love could not fill the void in her heart. She sat at the table and was unable to eat. She watched her husband's family grow while hers did not. Even Eli, the priest, did not understand.

What did Eli say in verse 14?

So why did God choose to expose Hannah's heartache in a meal setting? Why was it important for us to know that, in the depth of her despair, she could not eat? Why is it significant to realize that her drama continued year after year?

Please recall where our study began, in the garden, with the gift of food to enjoy. Remember the menacing plot to disguise God's gift, the gift that points us to the presence of God. For years, Hannah feasted on provoking words; she ate from the wrong tree. Then one day, her focus changed.

Something changed in Hannah's life after she prayed—after Eli blessed her. What changed before any circumstance changed? What changed before she conceived and before she gave birth to Samuel? (v. 18)

What was the result of Hannah's prayer? (v. 20)

Please read 1 Samuel 2:1–11. Take a few moments to consider how Hannah's prayer of rejoicing reflects the seasons of life mentioned by Solomon.

Hannah's new perspective came with settled peace in her heart. How does Hannah's prayer suggest she discovered how to enjoy God's gift?

Please write Solomon's words found in Proverbs 4:7.

> Wisdom is the principal thing; *therefore* get wisdom:
> and with all thy getting get understanding.
> —Proverbs 4:7 (KJV)

Solomon understood the seasons of life—that day and night, there is a time for every purpose under heaven. He also understood that in every season, there is nothing better for man than to eat and drink and to *make* his soul enjoy good in his labor.

Our journey with the Lord is reflected in our conversation. To the extent that we know him, our voice mirrors his. As Hannah drew nearer to the Lord, her conversation changed, she ate, and she was no longer sad.

Solomon was the third king of Israel and was spoken of as the wisest man on earth. He was the son of David, whom was anointed by Samuel, Hannah's son. He was not a perfect man, but he sought to find wisdom and understanding. He was not exempt from trials or choices that lead him astray; nevertheless, in his wisdom, he wrote much of what he discovered.

Please read again Ecclesiastes 3:1–13.

 What did Solomon say in verse 13?

The gift is ever before us, the presence of God ever inviting us to enjoy. Taste and see that the Lord is good.

There is nothing better for a man, than that he should eat and drink, and that he should make his soul enjoy good in his labour. This also I saw, that it was from the hand of God.
—Ecclesiastes 2:24 (KJV)

THE KITCHEN SINK—ENJOY

Perhaps the most significant work in Solomon's life was to build the temple—the house of God in Jerusalem. His approach to a life of excellence presents itself in this magnificent building, with walls layered in cedar and gold. However, the temple was an empty shell until the glory and presence of the Lord filled its inner chambers. Solomon's plans started with a conversation and included a beautiful presentation. His plans also included order and thoughtfulness, as each stone was fashioned far from the temple site, leaving the noise and debris outside. When the project was complete, Solomon invited the Lord to come. Afterward, he celebrated with a feast to enjoy, celebrating the work of his hand.

Consider the hard work you have done in this Bible study as a preparation for the Lord. As you have challenged your attitudes, your traditions, and your conversations, you have fashioned stones for the Lord's dwelling place—your heart. Now it is time to invite him in.

Invite him into your heart, your kitchen, and your dining room.

First, leave the noise of this world outside. If it helps, step outside your home and set the world aside for a moment—just a moment. Then go into your kitchen, the place where you prepare meals, and pray. Invite the Lord into your kitchen. Invite his presence to fill the room. Invite his joy to fill your dining area. Invite his love to fill your heart.

You can do this; it simply takes a measure of faith.

For the house which I am about to build *shall be* wonderful great.
—2 Chronicles 2:9 (KJV)

Please review the next page to prepare for the Group Taste-and-See Experience.

Group Taste-and-See Experience

JOIN THE CELEBRATION: SAVORY SOUP

Congratulations, you have worked hard. You have walked through the garden, the wilderness, and toward the Promised Land in biblical culinary shoes, and now it is time to celebrate. Experience the shared joy at the table by cooking your meal together.

For his shared experience, each member should bring a vegetable, spice, or meat to class. Precut the meat and vegetables into thin strips or bite-size pieces. Bring your ingredient(s) in a bowl or platter for presentation.

As a group, sit around the table and use a tabletop cooker—such as an electric skillet, prepared fondue pot, or hibachi—to cook personal helpings of each ingredient. Place the cooked ingredients into personal bowls, and then cover the cooked ingredients with hot vegetable broth. Season your soup as desired. Enjoy.

DISCUSSION SUGGESTIONS

- How does this shared experience enrich the celebration?
- What else would be good to serve in this soup?
- How is joy different from enjoyment?
- How would this type of meal work for your family?
- As a celebration thought, what would you like to ask or say?

Group Taste-and-See
Experience Guidelines

The Group Taste-and-See Experience exercises provide a platform to experience and discuss the meal aspects of each chapter. These exercises occur five times, after every fifth lesson. To insure a successful experience, we recommend a reminder phone call, text message, or e-mail from the group leader prior to the event. If possible, predetermine the dates for each fifth lesson and have group members note the dates on the Contents page.

It is our hope that each group member will participate at a level that meets his or her economic and culinary experience. While some groups may form around an already foodie network of friends, others groups may be comprised of neighborhood moms—some who cook and some who do not—or university students who live in a dorm and meet at a coffee shop. Some may choose to explore new tastes and flavors in a distinct epicurean style, while inexperienced cooks may benefit from discovering the basics—with an intentional withdrawal from ready-made and take-out. Be mindful of those in your group. Offer support and assistance when necessary. Be creative. Pray.

Since groups will meet in a vast array of venues, preparations for the Group Taste-and-See Experience will require different setup and cleanup procedures. Groups should discuss and designate specific job assignments to responsible individuals. We recommend that a few back-up supplies be on hand in an effort to avoid last-minute confusion or stress, such as paper plates, paper towels, and plastic forks. Please see the following setup essentials for each Group Taste-and-See Experience session. Begin and end your dining times together with prayer. Invite the Lord to join you as you gather in his name.

Chapter 1: The Gift–Prepare Jam, Pesto, or Salsa

Display fresh, dry, and canned ingredients to taste and experience.

☑ Provide plates to display fresh, dry, or canned ingredients from each recipe.

☑ Provide small plates, napkins, and a fork for each group member.

☑ Provide beverages, or water and cups, for each group member.

☑ Provide chips, crackers, or bread to use in sampling the group's recipes.

Chapter 2: The Plan–Prepare Sauces or Dips

Compare the cost and flavor of fresh herbs to packaged products.

☑ Provide plates to display herbs, spices, and other ingredients from each recipe.

☑ Provide small plates, napkins, and a fork for each group member.

☑ Provide beverages, or water and cups, for each group member.

☑ Provide vegetables, bread, and/ or sausages to use in sampling the group's dip and sauce recipes.

Chapter 3: The Invitation–Prepare Bread

☑ Preheat the oven to bake or warm bread; select which recipes to bake on site.

☑ Provide serving dishes for the bread assortment presentation.

☑ Provide small plates, napkins, and a fork and knife for each group member.

☑ Provide beverages, or water and cups, for each group member.

Serve warm bread with condiments like jam or vinegar and oil.

☑ Provide butter, honey, or jams to use in sampling the group's recipes, or, optionally, sliced deli meats and/or cheese.

Chapter 4: The Table and Chairs–Prepare Appetizers

☑ Group members are to bring appetizers on serving platters.

☑ Provide small plates, napkins, and a fork for each group member.

☑ Provide beverages, or water and cups, for each group member.

Display and serve appetizers with a beverage.

CHAPTER 5: THE CONVERSATION–PREPARE SOUP

Provide a tabletop cooker, utensils, bowls, and a beverage for the final Group Taste-and-See Experience. Enjoy!

☑ Provide a tabletop cooker, such as an electric griddle or skillet, fondue pot, or hibachi. (One cooker per six–seven group members.)

☑ Provide a pot of simmering vegetable broth, 1–1½ cups for each member.

☑ Provide small bowls, napkins, and a fork and spoon for each group member. (Use the fork while cooking the ingredients.)

☑ Provide beverages, or water and cups, for each group member.

Scheduling Options Chart: Select a Study Schedule to Meet Your Needs

Chapter	Lesson Title	30 Week Class or Devotion Study ↓	25 Week Group Study ↓	15 Week Group Study ↓	10 Week Group Study ↓	5 Week Accelerated Group Study ↓
The Gift	Enjoy! It's a Gift	Week 1	Week 1	Week 1	Week 1	Week 1
The Gift	Do Not Open	2	2	Week 1	Week 1	Week 1
The Gift	Food Fight	3	3	Week 1	Week 1	Week 1
The Gift	Another Garden Tale	4	4	2	Week 2	Week 1
The Gift	I Want That Recipe	5	Week 5	2	Week 2	Week 1
The Gift	**Group Taste-and-See Experience**	Week 6	Week 5	Week 3	Week 2	Week 1
The Plan	Dinner with a View	7	6	4	3	Week 2
The Plan	Plans for Dinner	8	7	4	3	Week 2
The Plan	Patterns of Celebration	9	8	5	3	Week 2
The Plan	Wait for It	10	9	5	Week 4	Week 2
The Plan	Behold the Best	11	Week 10	5	Week 4	Week 2
The Plan	**Group Taste-and-See Experience**	Week 12	Week 10	Week 6	Week 4	Week 2
The Invitation	What is Splendor Without You?	13	11	7	5	Week 3
The Invitation	Please Come	14	12	7	5	Week 3
The Invitation	Come Dressed for Dinner	15	13	8	5	Week 3
The Invitation	RSVP	16	14	8	Week 6	Week 3
The Invitation	Save the Date	17	Week 15	8	Week 6	Week 3
The Invitation	**Group Taste-and-See Experience**	Week 18	Week 15	Week 9	Week 6	Week 3
The Table and Chairs	Where are You, Little Lost Lamb?	19	16	10	7	Week 4
The Table and Chairs	The Empty Chair	20	17	10	7	Week 4
The Table and Chairs	The Flavor of a Favor Luncheon	21	18	11	7	Week 4
The Table and Chairs	The Marketplace	22	19	11	Week 8	Week 4
The Table and Chairs	Crab Cakes and Bacon	23	Week 20	11	Week 8	Week 4
The Table and Chairs	**Group Taste-and-See Experience**	Week 24	Week 20	Week 12	Week 8	Week 4
The Conversation	Between a Rock and a Hard Place	25	21	13	9	Week 5
The Conversation	Dinner and a Blessing	26	22	13	9	Week 5
The Conversation	I Knew You's Come	27	23	14	9	Week 5
The Conversation	Stirring the Pot	28	24	14	Week 10	Week 5
The Conversation	It's Time	29	Week 25	14	Week 10	Week 5
The Conversation	**Group Taste-and-See Experience**	Week 30	Week 25	Week 15	Week 10	Week 5

Select a Study Schedule

For you convenience, select a study schedule that will work best for your class or group study.

The 30-Week Study accommodates those with a time-limited meeting period, such as a Sunday school class or home school group. With this schedule, the Group Taste-and-See Experiences allow separate occasions for fellowship, with opportunity to discuss and relate the lesson topics. We recommend this pace for those new to bible study or for those who might benefit from a more in-depth class time discussion. The material, however, will inspire and challenge the most seasoned Christian.

The 25-Week Study combines the last lesson of each chapter with the Group Taste-and-See Experience. Extra time may be required on the Group Taste-and-See Experience meeting days.

The 15-Week, 10-Week, and 5-Week Studies cover the same material; of course, there will be limited discussion time for each section within the chapters. Groups choosing from these study schedules should focus on the chapter topics during their class discussions rather than trying to review each question. The Group Taste-and-See Experience sessions are an integral part of the study. Remember to allow time for the Taste-and-See exercises during the last session of each chapter.

ABOUT THE AUTHORS

Kriss DeBaca finds her mission in the kitchen. With a background in restaurant management and hospitality, Kriss loves sharing and enjoying God's love through providing meals. "The LORD meets me in the kitchen, every day. God will go to any length to speak to us. He speaks to me through food."

Londie Phillips has a passion for teaching, writing and design. She worked many years in Christian education, and as an award winning costume designer, she authored *Storybook Costumes for Dolls*. Londie seeks to express God's joy and creativity in her designs and teaching. "My prayer is that God's goodness and a glimpse of his glory is seen in the work he has given me to do."

For where two or three come together in my name, there am I with them.
—Matthew 19:20 (NIV)